The Modern School Superintendent

The Modern

HARPER & BROTHERS PUBLISHERS
New York

School Superintendent

HIS PRINCIPLES AND PRACTICES

By Robert E. Wilson

Associate Professor of Educational Administration

Temple University

THE MODERN SCHOOL SUPERINTENDENT

Copyright © 1960, by Robert E. Wilson

Printed in the United States of America

FIRST EDITION

A-K

Library of Congress catalog card number: 60-5711

57748

Dedicated to those invincible board members, coquettish tax-payers, restless teachers, nervous administrators, nettled secretaries, cussing custodians, and errant pupils who perfected the demonstration method in teaching me what I failed to read about school administration.

contents

foreword

by John Guy Fowlkes, Professor of Education,
University of Wisconsin

Among six definitions of the word "theory" as presented by the text edition of *The American College Dictionary,* the following four seem particularly cogent to those concerned with educational administration. Theory is regarded as "a proposed explanation whose status is still conjectural, in contrast to well-established propositions that are regarded as reporting matters of actual fact," and then again theory is established as "that department of a science or art which deals with its principles or methods, as distinguished from the practice of it," and still further as "a particular conception or view of something to be done or of the method of doing it; a system of rules or principles," and also as "contemplation or mental view."

During the last fifteen years concerted effort has been made toward the development of a broader, deeper and sounder theory of educational administration. Among such works in this direction are: *Principles of School Administration,* by Paul R. Mort; *The Nature of the Administrative Process,* by Jesse B. Sears; *Administration in Profile for School Executives,* by Harlan L. Hagman and Alfred Schwartz; and *Administrative Behavior in Education,* sponsored by The National Conference of Professors of Educational Administration, edited by

Roald F. Campbell and Russell T. Gregg (with eighteen contributing authors).

It would seem that these works along with *The Art of Administration,* by Ordway Tead, would provide adequate guidelines for high level performance in the daily administration of local school systems. Such does not seem to be the case in light of the frequency with which the statement, "it may be good theory but it doesn't work in practice," is heard at any gathering of practitioners of school administration, especially among groups of local school superintendents. The apparent disparity between the theory of administration and its practice has been a matter of considerable puzzlement to the writer for many years, since it would seem that if theory won't work it is not good and should be revised.

The treatise here presented is the chronicle and testimony of a former practitioner of school administration who has turned theorist. In a sense this work might be described as a test case of "theory" of administration. It also might be called the theory of administration in practice, or a theory of administration which emerged from sound practice. Regardless of the label applied to this volume, it reveals graphically and realistically the joys and sorrows, trials and tribulations, challenges and obstacles which the present-day school superintendent experiences.

This work is written in lively and dramatic style and to the writer reflects the penetrating insight of the theorist along with the story of a competent practitioner. It is strongly recommended to both theorists and practitioners of school administration.

A new brand of school superintendency is emerging upon the American educational scene. Its advent may not be widely heralded; nevertheless, it is quietly, at times sporadically, and certainly unequivocally, becoming apparent to the seasoned spectator. It is with the basic nature of this new superintendency, the requirements it makes of those entering the profession, the opportunities it offers, and its techniques of operation, that this book is concerned.

Until recent years it has been almost impossible to delineate either the characteristics of the superintendent's job or the personal and professional attributes of the man holding the post. As a result, no clear-cut profile of the composite superintendency has been available to guide the individual who is contemplating the profession as a career. It is still difficult to accomplish such an analysis with a high degree of accuracy. Responsibilities of the office have crystallized to a considerable extent. Job descriptions can be written which specify its general functions. Yet today one finds superintendents whose endowments, approach, and methods of operation differ, but whose performances are appraised as creditable. It is still true that no single pattern of administration guarantees success in the superintendency. At the same time, it is possible for the experienced observer to identify certain emerging patterns of operation which are likely to be the most successful.

It is also becoming evident which characteristics of the

successful superintendent entitle him to be labeled as the "new brand."

In the first place, the new school superintendent is professionally prepared for his work. Most boards of education have abandoned the traditional practice of elevating the best teacher in the system to the superintendency. They have come to realize that good teaching service alone does not assure good administration any more than a good courtship guarantees a successful marriage. The new species of superintendent has acquired successful experience in the classroom and in subordinate administrative posts, but has gone ahead to specialize in public school administration on a graduate level, possibly to include internship experience. Frequently, he holds a Doctor's degree.

Secondly, he is a dynamic fellow, personable, healthy, tactfully aggressive, and a leader. He has discarded the blue serge, severe demeanor, and professional reserve in favor of contemporary raiment, friendly helpfulness, and congeniality. He is intently curious about people as well as ideas. He has adapted to his peculiar needs the tools of the salesman, the diplomat, the trial lawyer, and the gracious receptionist.

Third, the new superintendent is a utilitarian psychologist. He is a student of human nature and a deft manager of people. He has acquired a practical discernment of motives, of individual and group differences, and of emotions. Although he may have protected himself with a tough armor to resist critical barbs, he is capable of both sympathy and empathy.

Fourth, he is an all-round able person. He not only knows sound educational theory and practice, but he is comfortable with the banker, the welfare agent, the sports enthusiast, the plumber, at the ladies' afternoon tea, or at the Great Books discussion. He possesses the necessary qualities for success in several occupations, and unless he has been approached by at least one industry for a much more lucrative position, he doesn't qualify for the category of the new brand. The only reason he remains in the superintendency profession is that he is still motivated by the same humanitarian philosophy that led him into teaching originally.

Finally, he is advancing to better posts rapidly, perhaps with greater speed than is good for him or the school systems he serves. He has arrived early in a good position, and the opportunities for the best superintendencies in the country are ahead of him.

The demand for these new superintendents is limited only by their practical willingness to accept another position. Boards of education are scouring the land for their kind. What is better for young administrators, but worse for education, the demand will increase in the last half of this century. Excepting for major national catastrophe, the number of schools and pupils will increase at a rate unseen in the United States since the western movement. The urgent need for quality school leadership is being aggravated further by the higher regard with which citizens are viewing education and their increasing expectations from their schools.

In the nation's frantic search for enough teachers to staff those schools, the need for the school's leadership has almost been overlooked. Where are the leaders to be found? There are just two major sources of supply to meet the demand for school superintendents.

One source is the classroom, among the ranks of young men with promise of executive capacity. In fact, many young teachers are eying the superintendency with curiosity. Frequently, they are motivated only by the position's potential for improving their financial status. But what is the work really like? Is it worth the sacrifice of money and time to become prepared? What is the life of a superintendent? Do I have what it takes to be a success? Where can I get complete information about the work before I make the break from teaching?

Obviously, the only complete picture of the life and work of a school superintendent can be painted by those who have lived the life. This book seeks to paint the complete portrait, with details which are not ordinarily found in administrative textbooks, professional journals, or graduate courses. Those sources of enlightenment are doing an adequate job of equipping the prospective superintendent with a lofty philosophy and the technical know-how for operating the schools. As important as the housekeeping chores are—budget making, school-building design, state reporting, curriculum development, teacher certification, legal entanglements, lawn maintenance, *ad infinitum*—there is much more to the job. In fact, if the training stops at this point, the aspirant has not learned the major part of his role, or the part most likely to generate his ulcers.

The ulcer-producing characteristic of the superintendency often comes as a surprise to many novitiates whose concept of the work is clouded by musing upon the salary, prestige, and a fantasy of being the boss. This treatise is planned to help them "face it." Before venturing, they are entitled to know that the superintendency carries with it acres of headaches, long hours, family neglect, risk, loneliness, criticism, and good chances for a coronary.

The other sizable pool from which the needed superintendents for top positions might be recruited contains the hundreds of practicing school administrators who want to advance but have not yet found the magic key. This document also suggests possibilities that might open the door. Educational literature sometimes refers to this process as in-service training, and yet much of the current activity intended for this purpose only rattles the door. What is keeping it locked? What causes mediocrity and failure in superintendency?

The book proceeds from the observation that no incident has ever come to the author's attention in which a superintendent was asked to turn in his uniform because of his mechanical ineptitude for the job. An examination of the records would reveal a few cases of failure attributed to ignorance, lack of training, or assorted promiscuity. The in-between lines of newspapers and board minutes, on the other hand, tell numerous stories of superintendency casualties traceable to various causes, all of which could be lumped together under the loose classification of faulty human relations. And yet the bulk of literature available to date for training school administrators is devoted to "minding the store" or to the acquisition of conceptual attitudes, with only a paucity of information designed to help them learn how to direct human action.

"Human relations" encompasses a host of activities, perhaps 90 per cent of the good superintendent's total operations. After all, about the same percentage of his day is spent with people —teachers, office personnel, pupils, parents, board members, salesmen, and a miscellaneous collection of residents. The effectiveness of superintendents in this area separates the successful ones from the mediocre.

The teaching technique used herein is that of principle supported by actual examples gleaned from intimate acquaintanceships with successful superintendents. The principles are fortified by the author's thirteen years on the school administrative firing line in five large and small school systems, as superintendent, assistant superintendent, principal, director, department head, and fiscal officer of a board of education; and they are mellowed by teaching experience in the public schools and the university. This approach is a deflection from the true clinical approach in which students are urged to analyze a situation and arrive at the correct solution. While this exercise has value, it ofttimes leaves out the salt of practical experience.

Admittedly, it is not possible to prescribe panaceas for all the potential problems an administrator will face, any more than it is possible to arm a teacher with all the methods which he will need; still, struggling superintendents, like future teachers, can find considerable guidance in knowing how experienced people have dealt with specific problems. Perhaps another superintendent cannot always adapt a technique used successfully by one administrator in a given situation, yet the familiarity with that technique will probably be of more value to a beginner than a pedagogical principle which is difficult to translate into action. Moreover, the book is limited to those administrative activities in which it has been observed that most unsuccessful superintendents have met their respective Waterloos.

Although it is envisioned that the thoughts contained herein will capture the attention of board members, citizens, teachers, professors of educational administration, superintendents, and subordinate administrators, the message seeks foremost the interest of those who are potentially America's superintendents of the future.

The new brand of superintendent needs company. It is hoped this book will help to provide it.

ROBERT E. WILSON
Temple University

The Modern School Superintendent

chapter one

Where You Can Go

IN THE BEGINNING THERE WAS . . .

The detailed history of the evolution of the American school superintendency, complete with play by play commentary, is yet to be written. It is doubtful that the complete story will ever be brought to light. Too many facts remain unrecorded in the sluggish but sometimes dramatic developments that took place in hundreds of communities throughout the nation as boards of education worked with insularity toward the establishment of the position.

The existing chronicles of the superintendency's origin skip from the early colonial experiments to the mid-nineteenth century struggles of growing cities to systematize their school systems, and then on to the maturation of the job during the present century. Whatever happened in the inbetweens is probably buried forever in the minds of those who actually wrestled with the objective. It is also probable that those involved in the early developments were unaware of the eventual significance of their efforts. Creating the post of school superintendent was apparently unworthy of recording for posterity.

Records do reveal several outstanding and isolated activities that were instrumental in the successful establishment of the position. This section will of necessity, therefore, deal only with these notable developments in the saga. A knowledge of the historical creation of the office is of value in helping the practicing superintendent to understand present-day public attitudes toward him.

The position of school superintendent is a product of growth and necessity. It was fashioned; it was not born. It unraveled; it was not conceived. No great architect envisioned a problem and designed a quick solution. Rather, the problem of administering in an organized manner the new, ambitious, and growing dream of educating all youth was attacked on many fronts by many citizens. As a model began to take shape in large cities concurrent with the Civil War era, it was copied indiscriminately by smaller communities in succeeding decades. By the turn of the twentieth century, the superintendency enjoyed almost universal acceptance. Not until this century has serious attention been given to its rational direction.

FOR NOW AND EVER SHALL BE . . .

As one analyzes the beginnings of the school executive role in the United States, he is inescapably impressed with two dynamic truths. One is the unchangeability of man's nature. The obstacles which delayed the progress in establishing the position, and the factors that influenced its development, are identical with the conditions that either help or impede the superintendent's work today. The other outstanding truth revealed by history is analogous to the thesis of this book: just as the human aspects of the position and its environment were paramount in the creation of the superintendency, so do they determine success or failure in the performance of the job today.

As the experienced school administrator reads these pages of early history, he will find himself at home with the educational pioneers of a century and a half ago.

Superintendency Began on Two Major Fronts

The position of superintendent developed primarily from common efforts operating on two separate fronts. On one front there was the movement to create the superintendency at the

state level, working downward through intermediate levels to
the local school head. On the home front, local boards of education were working independently to figure out how the
schools could be looked after if the town committeemen would
step out of the picture. Neither group had provident approaches
to the problem, but they felt their way along gingerly.

The early states participated in the development of school
administration through the tenth amendment to the Constitution in 1791, which set forth the principle that any powers not
mentioned in the Constitution were automatically delegated to
the respective states. This amendment has been the authority,
or excuse, for the state's assuming the responsibility to conduct
many civic functions, not the least of which was education.
As citizens began clamoring for provisions by which all
children could be educated, the state legislators responded by
enacting laws which would permit it, and by parceling out tidbits of money to enable it.

As soon as the matter of money appeared, it was only natural
to expect the lawmakers to do something about accounting for
it. Someone must be assigned the duty of checking on how
school districts were using the money. At first schools were
required to submit a statement of their financial activities—
probably the first state report demanded of local school districts. The answer to problems, even in those days, seemed to
be to appoint a committee. Thus was born before the nineteenth century the forerunner of a state board of education.

As more communities took advantage of the state funds, the
work load became too heavy for an appointed-volunteer board
to handle. Committee members looked around for a paid officer
to do the leg work of checking, reporting, and auditing. Sometimes the chore was palmed off onto an existing state officer, the
treasurer or the auditor. Administering the state's responsibilities for public schools was considered a lesser task which
an officer could look after with his left hand while his right
hand was attentive to more significant duties. As more and
more communities entered the educational arena, the state

officers wished to be relieved of this growing annoyance altogether.

State Superintendency Established

New York State lays claim to the first appointment of a state superintendent of schools in 1812. The practice spread rapidly to other states, and was accepted by new states almost as quickly as they came into the Union. Methods of selecting the state superintendent have always varied among the states. Some superintendents are appointed by the governor, while others are chosen by popular election. In some states the superintendent is selected by a state board of education, members of which may be elected, appointed, or chosen by a combination of both processes.

On a state level the office of superintendent of schools has seldom constituted a position of strong influence on education but has remained primarily a reporting center. With the exception of the famous Horace Mann in Massachusetts and Henry Barnard in Connecticut, along with a few other state executives who became significant forces for education because of their personal zeal and personalities, not as much leadership has been forthcoming from the position as educators have hoped. Such will probably always be the case, as perhaps it should be. The strong American conviction that the control of education should remain in local hands will undoubtedly prevent any sizable authority ever being granted to a state office. To do so would be to eliminate the basic ingredient that has made American programs for educating all youth stronger than any conceived at any time in any land. Although there are periodic urgings to appeal to state and federal governments for more legislative action and financial support, the public school system is one of the few remaining oases of resistance to the centralizing trend in American society.

This is not to deny the need for a state school-administrative office. After decades of sifting various ideas to determine the proper role of the state superintendency, there seems to be a general settling on the attitude that it can best serve education by providing information to school systems through its facilities of research, by stimulating educational improvements through its power of enforcing minimum standards, and by equalizing educational opportunities among school districts through a distribution of state moneys.

Growth Produces Another Kind of Superintendent— Intermediate or County

Accompanying the rapid westward movement in the United States during the first half of the nineteenth century, there developed hundreds of small local school systems, some organized on a township basis, some as a town, and some as more or less of a trading area. The task of visiting these numerous schools to inspect progress, use of funds, quality of teachers, and curriculum became impossible for a single state officer or committee. Gradually the responsibility was delegated to area committees, who, in turn, discovered that it required more time and knowledge than untrained laymen with their own livelihoods to earn could afford for the job. It was only natural, therefore, that a regional supervisor would become necessary.

These "assistant" superintendents were primarily middlemen for the state superintendent in gathering reports from local areas and in conveying his directives to individual schools. Since the county system of government was already established, it was natural that the county would become the definitive organization for appointing an "assistant superintendent" for the state superintendent.

County governments went through the same process as did state governments in handling the pesky but persistent matter of

school administration. County legislative bodies at first delegated the responsibility to an established county officer, who
inevitably discovered that he had neither the time nor ability
to handle this specialized type of service. Thus, the county
commissioners solved the problem by creating the position of
county superintendent. More than a dozen states had adopted
the pattern of county supervisory districts with county superintendents as the administrative officers before the Civil War.
Today, all but fourteen states employ the system to administer
school affairs in rural areas, approximately three thousand
intermediate superintendents being reported in 1957.[1] In those
fourteen states the county is the only administrative unit for
education throughout the state, and the county superintendent
acts in the capacity of a local or city superintendent. With these
exceptions, and the isolated cases of dominant personalities
who make their influence felt in educational circles, the position of county, or intermediate, superintendent continues primarily as a contact medium between the state and the local
school districts.

During the past quarter century there has been observed a
pronounced trend toward building fewer and larger school
administrative units. This tendency was the result of improved
means of transportation and of the need for consolidation in
order to equalize children's educational opportunities in districts with unequal financial abilities. The movement has also
been augmented by the realization that larger districts can
provide a broader training program at less cost than can
several small competing districts. In the twelve-year period
from 1932 to 1944 the number of school districts in the United
States decreased from 127,422 to 111,274, a reduction of
more than 1,000 per year! The present decade has witnessed
a squeezing down to fewer than 50,000. As this trend toward
fewer and larger rural administrative districts continues, the
county superintendent stands on the threshold of becoming
a significant officer for the first time.

[1] 1957 American Association of School Administrators, Official Report.

Grass Roots Movements
To Create the Superintendency

While states and counties were establishing their respective superintendencies, there was simultaneous action by local communities to find a workable device for administering their schools. Possibly because of the pioneer spirit of independence that caused men to take pride in doing things themselves, local efforts leading to the establishment of the superintendency were more lasting. These efforts were also responsible for building the status of the superintendent into the leadership role it has become in our society.

Local governing bodies were tardier, perhaps more reluctant, to turn over the management of schools to one individual than were their state and area counterparts, even though they were equally as conscious of the need for someone to "look after" the schools. The early councilmen, or more properly the selectmen, delegated the task to a school committee, sometimes comprised of a portion of the town's governing body and sometimes including other leading citizens who by their stature, or training, might know more about education. Frequently, the minister served on the school committee, since he was usually the most highly educated layman of the community. These committeemen actually visited the schools, saw to it that means were provided for paying the teacher, for having a place of meeting, and for supplying slates and books. They even evaluated the teacher's success by administering "standardized" tests.

Cities Appointed the First Superintendent

The need for the management function was felt first in the cities where a larger number of schools had been built than a volunteer committee could possibly oversee. This fact, coupled with the embarrassment of discovering that the learned masters knew much more about the processes of learning than did laymen, led the committeemen to the obvious conclusion that schools would be run more capably if they delegated the responsibility to someone better qualified for coping with the problems, and even paid him to do it. The files reveal that the Cleveland City Council in 1841, at a time when some people undoubtedly thought the council was off on a reckless spending orgy, dared to reimburse the person who was assigned this task one hundred dollars per year.

In reminiscing about these early starts, modern superintendents will be amused at the stereotyped characteristic of human nature as they observe the varying types of duties assigned these first local superintendents and the reasons for the assignments. Managing schools then, as now, encouraged two general classifications of functions: business and instruction. Then, as now, board members were willing for the superintendent to handle that phase with which they felt least secure, or for which they believed him to be the most capable. Apparently, most of the early committees felt the most bewildered in handling the instructional aspects of the enterprise. Either they assumed, as now, that there was something mysterious about dealing with a child's mind or that the teacher was not to be tangled with in her own den. Better to hire someone to look after the education and they, from their practical experience, would handle the business. This thinking is probably the origin of the practice of appointing the best teacher as superintendent, a custom still observed in a few small communities.

Other committeemen, perhaps better educated, didn't want to be bothered with the accounting trivia of school operations. They reserved for themselves the prerogative of inspecting the teachers and evaluating their success, and hired someone to "keep books."

The same oppositional attitudes exist today, among both board members and administrators. Reconciling the two points of view serves as another means of identifying the new brand

of superintendent. He is adept in both areas of school administration and, hence, performs both functions.

The introduction of the management function in education
can be likened to the innovation of a specialized position in a
modern city school system. For example, one of the tasks which
must be performed in every school, regardless of size, is the
employment of teachers. In a small organization, the chief executive interviews the prospects, makes necessary investigations, handles the paper work, and makes the decisions as to
which ones will be appointed, all in addition to performing
the usual administrative chores of the superintendent of New
York City; and perhaps he even teaches a class or two. He may
continue to employ all personnel in a system of 300 to 500
teachers. Eventually, however, the point is reached wherein
the number of persons involved requires an excessive amount
of his time. He must either neglect the other responsibilities or
engage assistance. Chances are that he will create the position
of personnel director with that specialized assignment. Early
school committees went through this same process to the inevitable conclusion that someone, call him a "superintendent,"
must be engaged to handle the growing specialized task of administering school operations.

Origin of the Title

At various times the person at the helm of the school system
carried the title of "Visitor," "Manager," "Treasurer," or
"Headmaster." Of the many possible titles that could have stuck
for the person destined to administer American schools, the
word "superintendent" fitted best. Combining the Latin words
super, meaning "over," with *intendo,* meaning "direct," answered the desires of the selectmen when they sought someone
to oversee and direct the operations of the schools. Unfortunately, the original connotation has lingered too long in the
minds of superintendents and board members. That modern

superintendents must direct and oversee school operations is still a major part of the position, but it leaves out what the new brand of superintendent considers to be an important element for his success—leadership.

It would be interesting, but unimportant, to know why, where, and when the word superintendent was first used. It will probably never be discovered, but for the benefit of the genealogically curious, the Massachusetts legislature in 1826 authorized the town committee to delegate to one or more of its members the duty of monthly or more frequent visiting "for the general charge and superintendence of all the public schools."[2]

It Wasn't Smooth Sailing Then Either

Watching the various pieces fit together in the evolution of the superintendency, it might be concluded that it was a simple, orderly, and logical process. Such was decidedly not the case, any more than was the organizing of the American public school system. During the century required for its establishment, the concept of superintendent met all shades of opposition, ranging from mild resistance to open hostility to periods of abolishment. The primary obstacles to its development are still existent in lesser degrees.

For example, many voices were raised in objection to the idea of appointing a superintendent on the grounds of cost. Economy-minded citizens opined that expensive overseers hadn't been necessary in the past, and they saw no reason for the luxury now.

Human emotions fought the innovation of a manager more than any other single factor. On the one hand, school committeemen distrusted the plan of having a specialist usurp their prerogatives. Cries of "one-man rule" were heard. Some

[2] Henry Suzzallo. *The Rise of Local School Supervision in Massachusetts,* Contributions to Edu., Vol. I, No. 3 (New York: Teachers College, Columbia, Univ. 1906), P. 144.

thought such a move would take the responsibility out of the hands of the people who supported schools. Conscientious board members worried that they might be shirking their obligations.

Teachers and principals also subverted the scheme openly and behind the scenes. They said that no one man, regardless of whether or not he had once been a teacher or principal, could understand their viewpoints. Principals were more active in fighting the establishment of a superior officer, just as they had been resisted strongly by teachers in the earlier struggle to appoint building principals. By the time of the Civil War, principals, relieved of teaching duties, had become firmly entrenched in most city school systems. Now they displayed sufficient strength in many communities to prevent boards of education from giving the new superintendent authority over them. In numerous instances they continued to have direct access to the board, with the superintendent being granted limited duties of accounting and reporting.

Considerable stumbling occurred also because no one knew what the function of the superintendent should be. There were no patterns. As experimental cities dared further to invade the vested interests and to establish the superintendent as executive officer of the entire school system, smaller communities copied the pattern.

An equally strong obstacle to its progress resulted from the fact that no one was professionally equipped to perform the task. Universities did not attempt to provide specialized training for the preparation of superintendents until long after the position had become established in the twentieth century. Early superintendents and boards earned substantially more fame for their pioneer spirit of exploration than history has yet given them credit for. They took their master teacher or principals and blazed paths through trial and error to the point where twentieth century professional educators could take over the assignment of giving direction and purpose to the training and performance of superintendents.

Still another obstacle to the speed with which stature was built into the position, and which has continued as a deterrent until the present decade, was the unwillingness of boards of education and communities to recognize the importance of the superintendency enough to assess it with a dollar value commensurate with their expectations. The history of public education support is marked with the attitude of getting the most results from the least expenditure. This unrealistic dream was no less applicable to the superintendency. Only since World War II have large numbers of boards realized that if they are to secure from their executive the kind of service they want, they must make the position sufficiently attractive from a financial viewpoint.

Where Are We?

There is still extensive fumbling and exploration in arriving at the mission and methods of operation for the superintendency position. Probably the most exhaustive and expensive study of administrative behavior ever attempted, the current research of the various Council of Professors of Educational Administration centers, has emerged thus far with only one clear conclusion, viz., more research is needed. Nevertheless, the superintendency has achieved the status of universal acceptance. Nowhere is there to be found any doubt as to the need for the services which the superintendent can render, with the possible exception of that found in the minds of a few highly theoretical and scattered educators, who envision complete equality for all school personnel. Even teachers who don't like the superintendent recognize the need for his position.

Today there are over 14,000 men and women filling the position of superintendent in the United States, with approximately 4,000 holding the office in urban communities of over 2,500 population. Every school system in the land has its chief administrative officer, although the title still varies among states. The nomenclature of superintendent is used in all cities and counties and for nearly all state heads.

Superintendents Organize

One proof of the arrival of any group of American people is its decision to organize. Before the close of the Civil War, school heads organized themselves as the National Association of School Superintendents with representation from nine states and twenty cities. It affiliated with the National Education Association at their Cleveland Convention in 1870 as the Department of School Superintendence. The organization changed its name to American Association of School Administrators in 1937 during the New Orleans Convention, and currently boasts a membership of over 11,500, one of the larger departments of the National Education Association.

National meetings have been sponsored almost continuously since 1866 in a bootstrap effort to determine goals, exchange ideas, and upgrade the profession. Membership is so large and diverse that numerous subgroups of superintendents have been organized to deal with problems peculiar to schools of similar size or types of responsibility.

Universities Offer Special Training

A final proof of the acceptance of the superintendency as a permanent and distinctive fixture in school operations occurred when universities undertook to improve its quality by organizing preparatory courses of instruction. Since these earliest efforts to professionalize the position, after the turn of the present century, graduate courses in school administration have become standard menu for approximately three hundred universities which offer advanced work in education.

That most of the preparatory courses have been geared to housekeeping chores of administration is natural in view of the comparative newness of the venture, and because the universities have generally followed the procession rather than led it. They can only look at what superintendents do and concoct courses that will help them to do it better. Where visionary professors have dared to lead, too often they have lacked the necessary proximity to know thoroughly what superintendents do on the job; consequently, they have built their courses on philosophical and sociological concepts. It cannot be questioned that a university has an obligation to elevate human sights beyond mundane affairs, but this book seeks to fill in some measure the void that has been left between philosophy and routine administrative chores.

Advantages of the Superintendency

In the remainder of this chapter the cleanest linen will be spread before the prospective superintendent in order to demonstrate the merits of considering superintendency as an occupation. The soiled linens will be hung out for airing in Chapter 2 and succeeding discussions.

The principal advantages are those which are apparent to any onlooker: higher income, prestige, greater opportunities for leadership, freedom of movement and decision, and the privilege of practicing the management function. The intangible satisfactions which a superintendent might gain from rendering service to mankind are no more than those derived from other levels of educational endeavor.

SALARY

The superintendency constitutes the most lucrative device by which a person engaged in education can barter his talents. The position of superintendent of the Cleveland public schools has increased in value from $100 per year in 1841 to $25,000 in 1958. An ambitious administrator can nowadays set his sites on the most financially rewarding educational post in the nation, that of the Chicago superintendent of schools, which would pay him up to $42,000. Or he might shoot for second prize in New York City at $35,000, or settle for Los Angeles at $34,000. There are 38 urban superintendencies that will pay $20,000 a year or more. In the United States 432 cities with 30,000 population or more, not including several smaller but wealthy suburbs, are paying their superintendents more than $10,000 per year, a livable income even with mid-twentieth century inflation. Superintendency salaries decrease according to the size and wealth of the school district, but whatever the amount, it still is the highest paid educational post in that system. A summary of financial opportunities is shown in Table I.[3]

TABLE I
MEDIAN SALARIES OF SUPERINTENDENTS OF SCHOOLS (1956-1957)

Population Group	Median Salary	No. of Systems Reporting
Over 500,000	$22,000	18
100,000 to 500,000	16,000	110
30,000 to 100,000	12,700	350
10,000 to 30,000	10,056	836
5,000 to 10,000	8,493	721
2,500 to 5,000	7,524	416

The value of the largest superintendencies in the nation as measured in dollars paid for their service is greater than that of the president of the largest university. The median salary of superintendents who serve in the smallest category of urban communities, between 2,500 and 5,000 population, was $7,524 in 1956-1957, higher than the median salary for full college professors in the same year ($7,076). Arguments can be presented for and against the justice of these comparative values, but they will not detract from the fact. The odds are better than fifty-fifty that the ratio will favor public school superintendents even more in the second half of the century.

[3] National Education Association Research Bulletin, Vol XXXV, No. 2, April 1957.

PRESTIGE

Despite the public maulings given the superintendent as described in succeeding chapters, the position, and usually the man, enjoys a posture of respect in the community. As head of the school system, which likewise claims general approval by the citizens, he represents education's summit within the normal community. As such, he is invited to occupy a seat of honor at community festivities, and at many private shindigs, alongside the minister, the mayor, and the president of the bank, of the country club, or of the community's largest industry. He is asked to "say a few words" at most such occasions, not because the audience is panting for his wisdom but because he represents the community's best efforts for acquiring wisdom. Frequently, his stature exceeds that of the mayor, who may have risen from an ordinary environment but who happened to get more votes than other candidates. Unless the minister is of unusual caliber, the superintendent towers over him in public awe. Even the town millionaire may be a scalawag whose status is dependent more upon money than brains, character, or contribution to the public good.

The socioeconomic status of the superintendent is much stronger in the socio than the economic. The fact that his stature throws him into frequent association with men of substantially greater income actually diminishes his income. He is expected to keep up with the Joneses in home, clothes, travel, and social whirl to an extent which his income cannot afford. It can be thrown in here as part of the cover charge that many of those same Joneses who expect and enjoy his companionship would be the first to protest an increase of salary for the old boy.

In many cases his prestige also exceeds his intellectual level. For some unrealistic reason, possibly a carry-over from the days when the headmaster was the most erudite man in the community, people expect the superintendent to know everything about everything. To the layman, education is education, as a tree is a tree. They forget that even a tree has dozens of branches and thousands of leaves, and that each tree specimen has numerous cousins. They rarely think of the superintendent as a specialist in a particular line of work just as they are. This can be embarrassing until the superintendent resigns himself to a moldy but pragmatic definition of education that entails not so much knowing the answers but knowing where to find them.

For some men who like it, there is prestige, too, in having a private office, a secretary, private telephone, name on the door and on the stationery, in wearing daily a suit and white collar, and in hobnobbing with a respectable class of people. While these may be inconsequential values, a man considering superintendency as a career is entitled to know they go with the job.

The superintendent not only exemplifies learning, for which the majority of people have a commendable respect, but he is also looked upon as the person who is "building for tomorrow," who does what he does because of desire to render service to humanity, who typifies the community's desire for morality second only after the minister, and who is the head of an organization, a goal which commands respect from the American inclination to worship leaders and heroes.

FREEDOM OF MOVEMENT AND DECISION

Practicing superintendents who are more conscious of the restrictions placed upon their actions and decisions will raise eyebrows at the inclusion of this characteristic as an advantage to the position. That is only because they have not recently compared their status with that of other members of the profession.

It is true that the nature of a superintendent's work and social pressure impose limitations upon his actions. He may also have to put in many more work hours than any other employee of the board of education. But in order to appreciate his relative freedom, he must reconsider his opportunities to attend professional meetings, to get away from his post for meetings during the day, to avoid the necessity for reporting in each morning or checking out at the end of the day. He is responsible in the final analysis only to the board of education, the members of which are seldom around enough to know what he is doing. Of course, he obviously rates low in comparing his freedom with college teachers or local businessmen, but within the public school system he ranks the highest in this respect.

The position also offers the opportunity for making one's own decisions with odds favorable for getting them accepted. Moreover, he enjoys the most gratifying thrill of free men—the right to rise or fall on his own decisions. Men with weak stomach for risk will not be happy in the superintendency. On the other hand, a man who can't abide having a superior officer breathing down his neck or having to clear with the boss before putting his decisions into action might enjoy the work.

OPPORTUNITIES FOR LEADERSHIP

The leadership potential for a superintendent of schools is obvious and almost limitless. Not only is there the opportunity to demonstrate leadership powers in building an outstanding educational program, but the superintendent may play an equally important role in guiding civic affairs, cultural development, morality, recreation—in fact, nearly any activity that society considers desirable.

Some superintendents don't take advantage of their leadership position to make worthwhile contributions. Others don't relish that much limelight, or the risk that is involved for one who leads. However, for the person who has the necessary qualities for leading and who thrives on it, the public school superintendency offers bountiful opportunities. As will be observed throughout this volume, the modern successful superintendent is in the forefront of educational advancement as well as community progress.

THE MANAGEMENT FUNCTION

The superintendency does not offer the only opportunity in education for exercising the management function, but it is obviously the highest level within the school system, if not the entire community. His work involves the management of people, things, and ideas, all the factors that any manager could oversee.

In recent years management has been recognized as a distinct trade necessitating identifiable skills. When applied to managing a school system, it entails most importantly the art of manipulating human beings. Planning, economics, law, engineering, logistics, as well as education, are included in the responsibility, but above all the management function involves corralling all these knowledges into an orderly process of getting a job done *by people*.

Importance of the Superintendency

A professor of education, noted for his interest in curriculum, was asked why he regularly attended the annual American Association of School Administrators' Convention, not noted for its concern with curriculum. His reply was flattering and challenging to practicing superintendents. "I have become convinced that if there is to be any progress in curriculum improvement, it must come through the superintendents of the nation. I want to get to know them personally. I'm discouraged with working through teachers' committees and college students. The superintendent is in a position to block change or to promote it."

Notwithstanding legal limitations placed upon the powers of the school superintendent, public restrictions that temper his decisions, and boards of education that want to run the show, the superintendent possesses enormous influence. Today most boards won't take action without the recommendation of the superintendent. From a practical operating point of view, therefore, he has authority over:

1. Who may teach.
2. Salaries of those who teach.
3. What is to be taught.
4. How it is to be taught.
5. Equipment and supplies that will be used to implement teaching.
6. Textbooks to be used.
7. What facilities will be built.
8. Where facilities will be located.
9. What school buildings children will attend within the district.
10. Hours and days of attendance.
11. Safety and sanitary conditions for school children.
12. Regulations governing the conduct of students from the time they leave home in the morning until they return.

Should one reflect seriously upon the significance of each one of these powers, multiply it by the 14,000 superintendents in the land, and consider that the powers extend to 1,000,000 teachers and 35,000,000 young people each year, one can begin to conceive the gigantic strength of this body of men. The importance of proper selection and training of every superintendent becomes obvious.

chapter two

What It's Like

What does a superintendent of schools actually do? How does he spend his day? His week? His year? What happens behind the closed door?

No one can answer these questions except a person who is, or has been, a superintendent of schools; not a teacher, not a board member, not a staff member, not even his wife. His secretary would have the most complete picture of the real function of the position, but even she is near the scene of action only when he is in his office. And no one can prescribe, nor can one pursue, a proper course of preparation for any occupation without knowing the exact nature of the position.

In this chapter the prospective superintendent will be given an orchestra seat for the most common goings-on of the superintendent. Even this work will not cover all of his activities. Those duties described herein have been assembled through intimate acquaintanceships with many superintendents, as well as from personal experience as an administrator in school systems of various sizes.

The popular notions of the superintendent's duties are obtained from textbooks, periodicals, newspaper accounts, and sporadic personal contacts. Such sources of information would lead one to the conclusion that a superintendent passes the time philosophizing upon education and the state of youth, in planning an on-going curriculum, deciding how a financial pie should be cut, making awards, shuffling papers, supervising a teacher's handling of a learning unit, erecting a building, running a meeting of the board of education, and occasionally firing a coach. That he does all these things is true. To assume that this is the substance of his work load is grossly misleading.

If one were to stop persons on the street and solicit their opinions on the nature of the superintendent's job, he would get answers relating to one or more of the above topics, plus one other incidental function if those questioned happened to have had some direct dealings with the superintendent. The reason most citizens have only a partial or a distorted idea of the superintendent's work is that their conclusions are predicated upon one or a few brushes with him, directly or vicariously. The fabled blind men who developed seven different conceptions of an elephant by touching seven different extremities of the beast had a cinch; there are hundreds of aspects to the superintendent and his work. A cartoon in a professional journal recently depicted a school superintendent as a nine-pointed octopus, each tentacle performing simultaneously a different operation. It approached the truth.

What a Superintendent Does, According to Professional Sources

The efforts of educational administration's scholars to define the role of an administrator are of remote value to the person who is seeking hard facts about what he might be doing day by day if he were a superintendent. These studies fall short in at least two respects. In the first instance, the pedagogical language glorifies the superintendent's duties to the degree of lulling him into thinking it's strictly a lovely, white-shirted, intellectual occupation. Who wouldn't be impressed with the prospects of spending his life performing the following duties which Tead[1] states are the essential elements of the administrative process?

[1] Ordway Tead, *Art of Administration* (New York: McGraw-Hill Book Co., 1951), p. 105.

Defining purposes and objectives.

Developing the broad plan for the structuring of the organization.

Recruiting and organizing an executive staff.

Delegating and allocating authority and responsibility.

Overseeing the general carrying forward of the delegated activities.

Insuring quantity and quality of performance.

Achieving coordination through committees and conferences.

Stimulating and energizing the entire personnel.

Evaluating the total outcome in relation to purposes.

Looking ahead and forecasting the organization's aims as well as the ways and means for realizing them.

Whose ego wouldn't be touched if he thought he could earn a living performing the following tasks which constitute the administrative process according to the recent studies of the Southern States Cooperative Program in Educational Administration?[2]

Defining needs and exploring problems.

Seeking information, determining resources, and providing consultants.

Proposing policies, formulating possible courses of action, and offering alternate proposals.

Initiating and implementing plans.

Evaluating progress.

Professional studies of the administrator's duties are also misleading in their oversimplification of the administrative process. Through an apparent attempt to condense the kaleidoscopic activities of the superintendent into a handy package for classification purposes, their conclusions are scholarly but highly generalized. For example, witness how simple this listing of the administrator's duties appears:[3]

[2] Southern States Cooperative Program in Educational Administration (Nashville, Tennessee: George Peabody College, 1954), pp. 102-105.

[3] John A. Ramseyer, Lewis E. Harris, Millard Z. Pond, and Howard Wakefield, SCDS Series, *Factors Affecting Educational Administration* (Columbus, Ohio: College of Education, Ohio State University, 1955), p. 20.

Setting goals.

Making policy.

Determining roles.

Appraising effectiveness.

Coordinating administrative functions and structures.

Working with community leadership to promote improvements in education.

Using the educational resources of the community.

Involving people.

Communicating.

Even practicing superintendents permitted this summarizing of administrative duties to slip by in their 1955 Yearbook of A.A.S.A.:[4]

Planning or the attempt to control the future in the direction of the desired goals through decisions made on the basis of careful estimates of the probable consequences of possible course of action.

Allocation or the procurement and allotment of human and material resources in accordance with the operating plan.

Stimulation or motivation of behavior in terms of the desired outcomes.

Coordination or the process of fitting together the various groups and operations into an integrated pattern of purpose-achieving work.

Evaluation or the continuous examination of the effects produced by the ways in which the other functions listed here are performed.

Scope of Superintendent's Jurisdiction

The list of activities in which a superintendent actually becomes engaged is virtually endless. Researchers striving to study the administrative process are deserving of sympathy, if not forgiveness, as they seek to condense duties into a workable list. They are always confronted with the dilemma that thou-

[4] A.A.S.A., *Staff Relations in School Administration* (Washington, D.C. The Association, 1955) p. 17.

sands of individual boards of education and superintendents determine in large part what a superintendent does. To cite all of the functions which all superintendents have performed in line of duty would require space equivalent to this book itself.

For the benefit of the prospective superintendent who wants to discover the problems and activities about which he must know something and do something, another listing is provided here. Admittedly, this is merely a condensed version, too. Each specific duty is suggested by only one word or phrase without attempting to elaborate upon the ramifications that might be involved in the performance of the duty. One needs to dwell for a few minutes on any one of the suggested duties to capture the breadth of the superintendent's function.

Superintendent's Scope of Duties

PERSONNEL:

Administrators, teachers, janitors, secretaries, bus drivers, cafeteria workers; medical, psychological, and specialized fields. Salaries, contracts, promotion, evaluation, morale, personal matters, dismissals, retirement, insurances, income tax, workmen's compensation, policies, sick leave, certification, equitable loads.

INSTRUCTION:

Kindergarten, elementary, high school, and some college. Content and methods of teaching art, business, economics, English, geography, history, home economics, industrial arts, mathematics, music, physical education, reading, science, spelling, vocational education, writing.

Reports to parents, grade promotion and retention, processes of thinking and learning, philosophy and history of education, cumulative records, legal requirements.

BUILDINGS:

Construction including costs, materials, design, excavating, bricklaying, carpentry, plumbing, heating, ventilating, utilities, lighting, painting, roofing, building codes. Sites and land-scaping, playgrounds, insurance, maintenance, equipment, legal aspects, educational adaptation.

FINANCIAL:

Receipt of money, accounting for it, spending it, raising it. Reports to board, public, and state. Budgeting, purchasing, taxation, bonds, legal requirements.

BOARD OF EDUCATION:

Legal requirements, powers, election, records, conduct of meetings.

DISCIPLINE OF PUPILS:

Legality, punishment, counseling, physical and psychological growth, methods of learning, motivation, attendance laws, work permits, suspension, expulsion, mental health.

ADMINISTRATIVE STAFF:

Personnel, principals, organization, psychological, relations to teaching staff, supervision, business administration.

SPECIAL EDUCATION:

Classes for orthopedic, hard of hearing and seeing, slow learning, fast learning, speech therapy, remedial. Psychological services, visiting teachers, guidance.

EXTRA CURRICULAR:

Athletics, music, dances, student council, variety of special interest clubs, school funds, recreation, yearbook, newspaper.

COMMUNITY RELATIONS:

PTA, citizens' committees, radio, newspaper, TV; service, civic, patriotic, and women's clubs; public speaking, cor-respondence, churches, parents, labor, chamber of commerce, law enforcement agencies, conducting campaigns, youth groups.

SPECIAL SERVICES:

Testing (ability, achievement, standardized, aptitude, indi-vidual); nurses, dentists, physicians, adult education, sum-mer school, welfare agencies, library.

HEALTH AND SAFETY:

Laws, fire, health department, traffic, police department.

CAFETERIA:

Diet, costs, personnel, reports, liability, purchasing.

SUPPLIES:

Textbooks, workbooks, numerous items for all instructional departments, janitorial, cafeteria, office.

EQUIPMENT:

Heating, lighting, ventilating, vehicles, athletic, maintenance, all instructional departments, office, furniture, audio-visual.

TRANSPORTATION:

Costs, bus capacity, reports, legal involvements, insurance, safety, roads, traffic, depreciation, liability.

RELATIONS TO ALLIED EDUCATIONAL INSTITUTIONS:

Colleges, professional organizations, private schools, parochial schools, professional journals and literature.

These are the tasks about which every superintendent must know something. These are the matters upon which any superintendent might be called to render a decision. The extent to which a given superintendent will personally perform the work suggested by each category and subtopic will depend upon the variables cited in the next section. Nevertheless, all superintendents must have knowledge about each function in order to assign duties, coordinate the whole process, and render decisions.

The Superintendent's Work Varies

No two superintendents perform identical functions, although all share some general duties and common goals. There appears on page 35 a lengthy list of actual problems which confronted one superintendent. Every superintendent will find in the list some problems with which he, too, has dealt. It is extremely unlikely, however, that another superintendent has experienced all of the same problems. One of the challenging aspects of the superintendent's work is that he never knows what situations tomorrow will bring.

The duties which a superintendent performs depend on several prominent variables:

1. Size of the school system.
2. Problems peculiar to a community.
3. The superintendent's relationships with the board, especially the confidence it has in his ability and judgment.
4. The superintendent's specialized skills.
5. The superintendent's primary interests.
6. The superintendent's nature and administrative philosophy.

SIZE OF SCHOOL SYSTEM AFFECTS DUTIES

Although the general responsibilities for administering the schools of New York City are the same as in Idaho's Xville consolidated rural district, there would be a substantial difference in the work day of the two chief officers. The bulk of the administrative functions in New York City are performed by assistants. In Xville the school head personally performs all the duties expected of a superintendent and also the functions of principal; he may also be the clerk-treasurer of the board of education, and he may teach classes a portion of the day.

The differences in the duties of two superintendents in a large and a small school system are similar to the differences between the functions of the president of United States Steel Company and the owner of a small metal processing plant just getting started. Both organizations have similar tools, machines, personnel, processes of operation, and goals. In the smaller plant the owner might sell the product, assist in its production, purchase the ingredients, keep the books, hire personnel, and compose his own advertisements. The primary responsibility of the president of United States Steel is to coordinate the efforts of a corps of staff specialists who actually perform the various services.

LOCAL PROBLEMS AFFECT DUTIES *5 7 7 4 8*

The allocation of the superintendent's time and energy also varies according to the imminent educational problems existing in different communities. Communities vary in themselves, a factor which dictates to a degree the time allocation of the superintendent's efforts. The problems demanding a superintendent's attention in a wealthy residential suburb where 95 per cent of the high school graduates attend an institution of higher learning are quite different from those found in a community with a per-pupil valuation of $2,000, or in a highly industrialized city, or in the small community with a university environment, or in a city with segregated schools.

The primary concerns in one community may be with overcrowded classrooms, while in another that of finding enough revenue to attract qualified teachers, in another that of low academic achievement, in another bickering religious factions, or in another a jet-propelled athletic program. While the common tasks as dictated by law, boards of education, and precedent are performed by the superintendent in each of these diverse communities, the extra duties are imposed by what people want and need at the moment.

SUPERINTENDENT-BOARD RELATIONS AFFECT DUTIES

Considerable space is devoted later on to the importance of the superintendent's developing proper working relationships with the board of education by separating the executive and legislative functions for operating schools. While the proposals suggested there may sound clear, the separation of functions is a matter of degree. A superintendent may be satisfied that he is performing the executive function, but the degree to which he has exclusive jurisdiction over administrative duties may be more or less than that of another superintendent who is also satisfied with his division of powers. Therefore, the precise nature of a superintendent's duties varies according to the extent to which a board has confidence in its superintendent to carry the ball alone. Likewise, the nature of his duties is influenced by the superintendent's and the board's interpretation of what constitutes executive action.

For a specific example, in one Midwest city the board of education examines each voucher at a regular meeting before the superintendent and the clerk are authorized to make payment. In a nearby city of approximately the same size, the clerk, with the approval of the superintendent, pays bills as they come due and the board merely sanctions the list of payments at its monthly meeting, occasionally challenging a voucher that seems questionable. At some meetings the latter board would, in effect, spend a quarter of a million dollars in less than a minute—the time required to initiate a motion, obtain a second, and to call the roll for voting. Both superintendents said they were performing the executive function. In the former case the chief executive was satisfied to have the board occupy its time with incidental financial matters, with the hope that board members would stay out of the important aspects of education. In the second city the superintendent thought the board should be involved, as they also wanted to be, in educational affairs. From a realistic attitude, there are arguments for both points of view.

There are boards even today who believe sincerely that they should meet every teacher before they pass judgment on her employment, that they should act on discipline problems, that they should visit classrooms to evaluate teachers, that they should read each textbook before its adoption, or that they should personally supervise the construction of a new building. The superintendents working in these school systems are, in some instances, pleased with the division of the executive and legislative responsibilities. As vital as the separation is, it remains a relative matter.

SUPERINTENDENT'S PRIMARY INTERESTS AND SKILLS AFFECT DUTIES

What a superintendent actually does in the conduct of his office is governed to a great extent by his personal skills and interests. One executive may consider himself especially adept at hiring secretaries, while another, whose interests lie more in the area of curriculum, will undoubtedly delegate the entire personnel function. Some superintendents, especially if they are ex-coaches, voluntarily devote a disproportionate share of their administrative time to athletic matters. A superintendent who was a former chemistry teacher may build an outstanding science course of study, much to the neglect of other instructional areas. Most superintendents leave the primary grades alone because they feel insecure on that level. There are a few whose major interest is looking for a better job, or gardening, or selling real estate, and hence delegate the major part of school administration to subordinates.

A SUPERINTENDENT'S PHILOSOPHY AFFECTS DUTIES

Human nature and administrative philosophy also influence what a superintendent does on the job. There are some insecure or overconfident administrators who lack the courage or good judgment to delegate duties, and who try to perform all the functions personally even in a sizable school system. This philosophy can have only three possible outcomes: a school system that neglects the complete servicing of pupils and teachers, a corps of administrative staff robots, or an early demise for the chief. One such superintendent, who suffered the latter result, refused to employ any assistants in a school system of more than fifteen thousand pupils, and even spent approximately half of his working day in visiting classrooms. While that limited phase of the system was in commendable condition at the time of his earthly departure, it required years for his successors to bring the educational program up to the standards of comparable cities. If such a man is unconcerned with his own physical well-being, he should at least have regard for his only reason for being in the position—facilitating the learning of boys and girls.

At the other extreme is the timid administrator who dares not move in any direction before "checking" with every segment of his educational domain, including the bus driver. Some do this in a frantic effort to comply with the professor's admonition to be democratic, while others have never quite been able to overcome the effects of early matriarchy.

There is also the type of superintendent who earns the title of "operator" in any occupation. He manages to con subordinates into carrying out all of his responsibilities while the board still thinks he is doing them; meanwhile, he conducts a merry race for office in some professional organization, or writes articles, or becomes engaged in any one of a dozen activities which have only remote connection with the performance of the job for which he was hired.

There are even some men at large in the superintendent's office of minor school systems who have been able to achieve that level of school service without ever having known the joy of a full day's toil. Less tactful appraisers might call them "lazy."

Distribution of the Superintendent's Time

Allowing for the variables in mode of operation cited above, it is impossible to designate what *the* superintendent's function is but only what *most* superintendents do. Surveys conducted among practicing administrators indicate similarity of duties as shown in Tables II and III. These studies also accent the point that duties depend upon conditions and the individual.

A common weakness of surveys is inherent in the control exerted by the framer of the questionnaire upon the freedom of the respondents to convey the complete story. A pollster

TABLE II
ACTUAL AND IDEAL DISTRIBUTIONS OF TIME
BY CITY SUPERINTENDENTS OF SCHOOLS, 1950[5]

Functions	Distribution of time	
	Actual	Ideal
Instructional leadership	23.7%	30.5%
General planning for program as a whole	17.1	18.2
Financial administration	15.1	10.5
Personnel administration	14.0	12.9
School-plant management	11.7	8.3
Public relations	11.1	12.2
Pupil services supplementary to instruction	7.3	7.4
Classroom teaching	0.03	0.01

TABLE III
PER CENT DISTRIBUTION OF TIME DEVOTED TO VARIOUS FUNCTIONS
BY RURAL SUPERINTENDENTS, 1950[6]

Functions	Per cent of Time
Instructional leadership	25.6%
General planning for program as a whole	15.5
Financial administration	18.1
Personnel administration	12.4
School-plant management	8.6
Public relations	9.5
Pupil services supplementary to instruction	10.0
Classroom teaching	0.3

shapes his questions so as to obtain the information with which he is concerned at the moment. Further limitations on the accuracy of many questionnaires result from the phrasing of the questions which may cause overlapping or inadequate delineation of specifics.

For example, a closer examination of the classifications of information sought in Table II will make it obvious that a respondent in trying to indicate the percentage of time devoted

[5] *The American School Superintendency*, A.A.S.A. 30th Yearbook, 1952. p. 293.
[6] *The American School Superintendency*, A.A.S.A. 30th Yearbook, 1952. p. 461.

to "general planning for program as a whole" would have difficulty separating this function from each of the other classifications. Again, a superintendent could be performing the "public relations" function while also administering finances, personnel, instructional leadership, plant management, and even classroom teaching. Or, personnel administration can scarcely be divorced from instructional leadership, finances, or pupil services.

In such a questionnaire, where would a superintendent include the time he spends on conducting a campaign for a bond issue, in straightening out a threatened strike by the custodians, in conducting board meetings, or handling complaints from parents, or the dozens of sordid episodes encountered in the managing of a school system which superintendents discuss in the unscheduled gatherings of their conventions?

Such a survey can only produce generalities. Furthermore, it is unlikely that any questionnaire can be contrived to reveal the extent to which specific duties vary from week to week and year to year. The listing on page 25 suggests the scope of his activities, but it does not reveal specifics. This is approached in the listing on page 35 which enumerates actual problems that received a good share of one superintendent's time during a three-year assignment in a medium-sized "average" city. This is not to imply that he was confronted with these same duties every three-year period of his administrative career, or that all superintendents would be faced with these problems. Undoubtedly every superintendent experiences some problems identical with those of his colleagues, while others could magnify the list. Moreover, the superintendent who submitted this list testifies that during the period he also performed the usual duties expected of the chief executive in managing a school system and minding the store.

These are the types of situations which develop in a school system to absorb a sizable proportion of the superintendent's time but which are rarely found listed in any professional treatise on administrative duties. No one wants them; little can be done to prevent them. Yet they must be handled. At the moment of their occurrence, their solutions are as important as any administrative duty stated in the refined sources of enlightenment.

The reader is urged not to skim through the list but to dwell upon each problem long enough to imagine the time, mental pressure, and skill which would be required to deal with it. Then he is invited to consider what professional course he has had, or is contemplating, that would prepare him to handle the situation. He should also reflect upon his own strengths and weaknesses to decide if he wants to make a career out of this sort of pastime.

Actual Situations Encountered by a Superintendent During a Three-Year Period

Established new boundary lines for city's elementary school districts.

Male teacher found guilty of sodomy with high school boys.

White girls of high school age dating Negro boys.

A local patriotic lodge demanded an investigation of all history books to determine extent of anti-American propaganda.

Jehovah Witness group requested use of school building for worship service.

Vandals caused over $3,000 damage to a school building.

Teachers' union pressured for an increase of teachers' salary maximum.

Sixty pupils suffered poisoning attributed to food consumed at school cafeteria.

A rival contractor publicly accused the school building contractor of faulty and hazardous workmanship.

Athletic booster club conducted stealthy campaign to have basketball coach dismissed.

Parent threatened suit against teacher who paddled a pupil.

Bottles of liquor found in high school boy's locker.

Board member insisted that the superintendent transfer a principal to another building from the one in which member's daughter was attending classes.

Received anonymous telephone call that bomb was planted in school building.

A PTA demanded that adult patrol guards be placed at street crossing in that district.

Junior high girls en route to school confronted by man guilty of indecent exposure.

A section of ceiling plaster fell, injuring a child.

Three parents protested because their boys were "kicked off" football team for smoking.

Janitor accused of writing indecent notes and leaving them in typewriters for students to find.

Purse containing $30 stolen from locker.

Junior high girl accused male teacher of molesting her.

Parents demanded that high school sororities be disbanded.

An assistant football coach submitted resignation in mid-season because of argument with head coach.

Local merchant protested to board of education the purchase of typewriters from out-of-town firm.

High school pupil skipped school and was injured in auto accident.

Parents refused on religious grounds to have child vaccinated according to board regulations.

Plumbers went on forty-two-day strike during construction of a building badly needed to relieve an overcrowded condition.

Melting furnace exploded in high school metal shop, hospitalizing a pupil.

A sudden annexation transferred 110 pupils into a school district where the building could not accommodate them.

Fight after football game resulted in jail sentence for three boys and numerous injuries.

Petition received from parents requesting dismissal of a teacher.

Receipt of needed supplies delayed because purchasing agent failed to place order after an argument with a principal who wanted the supplies.

Teacher filed suit against superintendent and board of education for "illegal" dismissal.

Group of students refused to pledge allegiance to flag because of religious convictions.

Jewish patrons protested Christmas observances in schools.

Principal unable to explain $190 shortage in his school funds.

High school students staged walkout from classes because school was not dismissed following Friday night's defeat of arch rival in football.

Merchants protested the schools' selling of tablets, pencils, and miscellaneous supplies.

Board member died, creating vacancy that had to be filled.

Epidemic of respiratory diseases resulted in 40 per cent absenteeism of pupils and teachers.

School officials responsible for planning and entertaining tri-state professional convention in city.

Citizen accused board member of being involved in illegal sale of equipment to school.

Changed entrance age requirements for admittance to first grade, thereby stirring parental unrest and some bitter objections.

Rowdy and disreputable student parties after Senior prom.

Parents objected to special classes for gifted children.

A sub-contractor filed lien against board of education funds for the general contractor's failure to pay the amount due the sub-contractor.

Teacher accused of advocating trial marriage.

Elementary teachers requested relief from noon duty.

PTA requested permission to sponsor bingo game at benefit party in school.

Board's finance officer innocently made error of $10,000 in financial report which was released to the public.

Social studies teacher accused of advocating communism.

Board member's daughter fails in college and blames "poor high school preparation."

Teacher wrote letter to editor of local paper criticizing a board's decision.

Ministerial association objected to the number of school activities that kept children out of church youth functions.

Tornado reported heading toward city during school hours.

Salesman discovered calling teacher out of classes for his "pitch" contrary to board regulations.

Shipment of floor wax found to be defective, resulting in damage to gym floors.

Neighborhood gang feuds erupted in school.

Dentists requested that children be dismissed during school hours for dental appointments.

During the three-year period the superintendent received 87 calls complaining about children crushing shrubs, lawns, and fences; 143 requests for students to participate in contests; and had reports of 340 windows broken in school buildings.

Length of Work Week

A sign found in many production plants reads, "Work hard eight hours a day, and some day you might be the boss and work twelve hours a day." The slogan is as applicable to educational work as to industry. Champions of the forty-hour week, or less, should avoid even considering the superintendency. According to the 1952 American Association of School Administrators study, superintendents around the nation average approximately sixty hours per week, distributed as shown in Table IV. It is interesting to note that the larger the system, the more hours per week are entailed. It should be pointed out also that if this is the average, many were putting in over seventy hours a week.

TABLE IV

AVERAGE NUMBER OF HOURS PER WEEK SPENT ON THE JOB
BY CITY AND RURAL SUPERINTENDENTS[7]

Average hours per week	City	Rural
Officially scheduled hours	42.6	42.4
Extra hours on office work	7.1	7.0
Meetings, dinners, etc.	5.0	4.3
Professional trips out of town	3.3	4.0
Total hours, on the average	58.0	57.7

Weeks per Year

The twelve-hour day for superintendents does not just apply
to the thirty-two or thirty-eight-week year which is standard
for teachers. Most superintendents in the larger cities have no
more than a month's vacation per year, many taking only two
weeks. Christmas and spring vacations mean nothing to these
men except a chance to reduce the "Things to Do" file. The
A.A.S.A. survey reported, "on a city-size basis, the median
days (of vacation) taken ranged from 12.5 in cities 50,000–
99,999 in population to 15 days in the cities 100,000–199,999
in population."[8]

Although superintendents still smart from the following
questions from citizens, even heard from teachers occasionally,
they don't try to explain any more: "What are you going to do
all summer?"—"Aren't you relieved school is over?"—and
about August, "Are you ready to go back to work?"—and in
December, "Where are you going over Christmas holidays?"
Should a superintendent try to explain all that he does during
the summer months, he would see the light of incredulity fire
up in his listener's eyes.

[7] *The American School Superintendency,* A.A.S.A. 30th Yearbook, 1952,
p. 452, 461.
[8] *The American School Superintendency,* A.A.S.A. 30th Yearbook, 1952.
p. 295.

The Typical Day is Harum-scarum

The most typical characteristic of the superintendent's day is its dissimilarity to the day before. Any administrative position with as wide a jurisdiction as the superintendency invites divergence. Any occupation dealing mostly with people can expect to be kaleidoscopic. Combine these two qualities into a single office and one has chaotic pyrotechnics, perhaps the most accurate terminology for describing the superintendent's typical day.

In order to work through this maze of activities to accomplishment, the superintendent must systemize his duties by setting aside certain times of the day for recurring certainties. Like any orderly executive, he should reserve a designated time for reading mail, for dictation, conferences, outside telephoning, paper work, school visitations, and the like. By letting his schedule be known as widely as possible, those around him will respect it. There are three obstacles to the smooth operation of this technique for the superintendent.

In the first place, there are enough developments during the day that qualify as emergencies to provide almost a continual parade of interruptions. Whether the superintendent be the head of a one-building system of 300 pupils or a 60-building organization with 40,000 pupils, there are too many people involved to avoid emergencies. Routine matters can be well handled by subordinates without bothering the chief, but any top executive needs to know about, possibly render decisions on, the unusual. Therefore, he can't ignore these developments to pursue his orderly plan for the day.

In the second place, people never let him forget that regardless of status he is still a servant of the public. As such, he is expected to be available *when* they want him for any of a thousand and one concerns of theirs. A good secretary, the most valuable employee a superintendent has, can sieve the calls in order to reduce interruptions, but she can't block them all. The modern superintendent has accepted the viewpoint

that every matter brought to his attention is a serious problem
to the originator. He also recognizes the typical citizen's attitude that the superintendent is still a public employee, meaning that he should be available to quench their thirsts.

Third, as a public servant and representing the entire school
system, the superintendent is called directly by many people
for insignificant matters that could and should be handled by
a teacher or subordinate administrator. There are those new
residents of any city who were accustomed to calling the superintendent about every educational concern in their former
rural environment. There are also those who subscribe to the
slogan that one should always "go to the Top" for an answer.
How ridiculous this can become is illustrated by a superintendent of New York City who reported that citizens have
called him directly to complain about the treatment of a child
in a Brooklyn elementary school, or to inquire what school
district they should send a child, or to report windows broken
by children on the way home from school.

Other Characteristics of the Superintendency

A POSITION OF RISK:

The public school superintendency is a position of risk. The
teacher who enjoys the protection which tenure laws provide
should weigh his values carefully before gambling with the
superintendency, which has little or no security. The 1952
A.A.S.A. survey revealed that more than half of the city superintendents had no legal tenure and 71 per cent of the rural
superintendents had none. While only a handful of superintendents have permanent tenure for that position, many do
have tenure as a teacher or administrator in the system. According to that same study, the median length of contract (assured tenure) was for only two years. More than one-fourth of
all city superintendents surveyed in 1950 served without any
written contract!

While some arguments are advanced periodically in favor
of offering tenure, or at least longer contracts, to superintendents, it is unlikely that such will ever come about. The
public has already shown its annoyance with guaranteed employment for teachers as well as for factory workers with sen-
iority rights. It is doubtful if any community will want to
cement its superintendent in office regardless of his quality.

The degree of risk involved in the superintendency is emphasized by the realization that most school districts have but
five school board members, and therefore it requires only three
citizens in the entire community, large or small, to "get down"
on a superintendent and he's through. The gamble is also spot-
lighted by the fact that the public is fickle. The most able
superintendent can have the rug pulled out from under him
by a relatively minor incident in the schools for which he may
not even be directly responsible. The case book reveals instances of capable superintendents being dismissed because of
having clashed with a popular coach, or a board member's
child having failed, of promiscuity among high school youth,
or of an unfortunate school building fire.

A POSITION OF PRESSURE

Succeeding chapters illustrate in more detail the kinds and
degree of pressures to which a superintendent is subjected.
Suffice it to summarize at this point that he is pressured for
time, by numerous opposing private interests, and by an un-
defined purpose for the office. Combine the characteristics of an
executive position, a public office, and an officer whose function is not clearly understood, and there will inevitably be
pressure on the person holding that mongrel office.

POSITION OF COMPULSORY EMOTIONAL CONTROL

"Laugh, Clown, laugh." "Grin and bear it." "Down, boy."
"Count to ten." "Steady as she goes." "Remember the wife and
kids must be fed." These are the warnings one would hear if he
were tuned in on the superintendent's emotional control

mechanism as he plods through the varied and pressured events of the day. He is compelled to maintain pleasant equanimity regardless of how he feels or how the day is going. He must typify the quiet dignity expected of the school superintendency, and he must try to keep enmities of the school system to a minimum. Moreover, preserving a composed, tranquil frame of mind is the only way in which he can continue to render sound judgment throughout the day. The excitable, temperamental individual will find exceptionally rough going in the occupation.

This compulsion for the superintendent to refrain from blowing his stack aggravates his physical and mental condition. It emphasizes the need expressed elsewhere for hobbies and for frequent escapes from the office in order to safeguard sanity as well as health. A sense of humor is one of the most essential tools in the superintendent's work kit.

A POSITION CAUGHT BETWEEN OPPOSING FORCES

As chief executive of a public school system with the scope of responsibilities which he carries, the superintendent is continuously caught between forces of conflicting demands. This point will become obvious again and again throughout this volume. How adroitly he dances in and out before the pincers close on him determines his success. It also makes obvious the qualities necessary for superintending a public school as described in Chapter 10. Try to visualize the skills involved in avoiding the vise of these oppositional forces:

A board of education driving for economy and efficiency against a corps of teachers wanting increased salaries, better working conditions, more supplies, and being motivated by humanitarian values.

An administrative staff checking and evaluating teachers who resent supervision and interference with "academic freedom."

Teachers pressing pupils for more strenuous efforts and higher standards of learning and conduct against students who don't even care if school keeps.

Coaches wanting more time off, more money, and lower eligibility requirements against Latin and English teachers concerned primarily with cultural developments.

Clashes between any two departments of school personnel: vocational education vs. college preparatory, elementary vs. secondary, custodians vs. teachers.

Teachers arrayed against parents for any of a hundred reasons.

Educational interests against public interests; what is best for the education of children vs. what the public will accept.

Legal restrictions on financial and other administrative decisions against common sense for solving a given problem.

Limited revenue against an endless parade of needs which never seem to be satisfied.

A POSITION OF LONELINESS

That a superintendent of schools is generally a lonely man comes as a shock to most people who are more conscious of his wide circle of acquaintances, his numerous activities in the community, and his spot in the limelight. A primary reason for his loneliness arises from the fact that he is absolutely the only man in the community who is engaged in his particular line of work. In a sense he works in isolation. He must leave town in order to share ideas and opinions with another person involved in the same type of occupation. It is true that he can and does consult with numerous individuals in the community to obtain counsel on various problems, but no one views a given situation exactly as a superintendent might do. Even the superintendent in a neighboring community will not be close to his particular situation.

His lonely status is aggravated by the fact that he dare not share his numerous confidences with anyone in the community. Superintendents who have made the mistake of confiding in persons whom they considered intimate friends soon discovered that much of their information amounts to voluptuous gossip which few people have the courage or loyalty to preserve unto themselves. For the superintendent to keep these matters bottled up is unnatural and harassing to the nervous system. Superintendents sometimes resort to confiding in out-of-town salesmen who have been good friends over the years. School supply representatives report that they waste many an hour in this diversion to relieve the superintendent's pent-up burdens. This practice, too, can become a costly mistake.

Eventually a superintendent discovers that the only safe course of action is to listen and not repeat. This becomes a whopping challenge as he meets with many friends in the community who seek to pump him for the "inside dope." As he parries and ducks these questions, he offends. Consequently, the superintendent finds himself *with* many friends, but not truly a part of the group. He remains a lonely man in the midst of hundreds of "friends."

A POSITION OF UNPLEASANTNESS

Perhaps the nature of the problems encountered by a superintendent already cited are enough to substantiate this point. Add to this consideration the fact that every decision a superintendent makes aligns someone against him, and the fact that he is frequently required to say "No"; and one emerges with a concept of superintendency quite different from that held by the teacher or the man in the street. Exactly what the ratio of unpleasantness to pleasantness might be has not yet been surveyed.

Neither is it known how much the factor of unpleasantness is responsible for the number of administrators leaving the position through illness, early death, voluntary transfer to teaching positions, leaving the educational profession altogether, or the turnover resulting from the persistent hope that the next position will be more pleasant. Apparently no one has worried sufficiently about these matters yet to gather statistics. The scattered studies on annual administrative turnover show that from 10 per cent to 25 per cent of the superintendents of the nation change position each year, especially among the smaller school districts. One study in Wisconsin indicated that 29 of the 54 administrators who left their positions in 1953-1954 did not obtain other administrative positions.[9]

Notwithstanding this dismal but accurate portrayal of the position, there are still fifty or more candidates for every good vacancy that occurs. There must be ways of working through the darkness toward a higher ratio of pleasantness and gratification from the job. That is what the remainder of this book wants to prove.

[9] *Administrator's Notebook,* Midwest Administrator's Center, Chicago.

chapter three

How to Plane a Board

Every superintendent of schools has entertained the thought at one time or another during his service that educational progress would be a breeze if it weren't for the board of education.

Although this abstraction is warranted on occasion, superintendents will admit in their objective moods that the venerable decision to conduct public education under the control of representative laymen was one of the fortunate happenstances for the nation's progress.

The board of education, sometimes called the school committee, or the school directors, has much in common with other types of governing boards throughout the land but also has some indigenous characteristics with which few citizens are acquainted. The board is like Congress, the legislature, the county commissioners, or city council in that in most states it is an elective body with statutable jurisdiction over a described area, but is unlike those bodies in that board of education members are normally elected on a nonpartisan basis and accept no remuneration. The board of education resembles the board of directors of an industrial company in that they both operate under a legislative-executive process, but differ in the source of their respective powers, salaries for service rendered, motives for decision, personal investment in the organization which they represent, and usually the technical knowledge about the nature of the work on which they are making decisions.

A board of education shares similarities with a charitable or welfare board in respect to remuneration, limitation of powers, and motives for decision, but is dissimilar in method of selection, scope of influence, and regulation of their activities. A board of education is akin to many community governing bodies elected to perform a civic task, but is unique in that the board member rarely receives any thanks for his public service and mostly gets a fusillade of complaints.

A board of education is simply a group of five, seven, nine, or as high as nineteen, persons, selected from and by the citizens of a geographical area to look after the education of children in that community. It has absolute and final authority over the operations of the public schools in that area *within* the powers that have been delegated to it by state law. This latter point needs emphasis. While the board's powers are final, they can be considered only tentative since the board's actual being may be dissolved by a greater power—the state. Responsibility for public education belongs to the state, but every state has delegated its responsibility to local communities. The state created the system of organization for operating public schools, assigned the governing bodies certain duties to perform, but reserved the right to disband the organization or retract the power to perform the duties at any time. Professional literature and the law refer to the organization of a school district as a quasi-corporation; it is a corporation but it isn't.

How Board Members Are Selected

In general, the only criterion for becoming a member of a board of education is the securing of more votes than other candidates. 95 per cent of all board members in the United States are chosen by popular vote,[1] the majority of whom are elected on a non-partisan ballot.[2] It is encouraging to note that

[1] Alabama and Pennsylvania provide for appointment of board members in a few districts.

[2] Elected on partisan basis in Alabama, Connecticut, Florida, Louisiana, Rhode Island, and Pennsylvania.

in 43 states board members are now elected "at large" rather than by area representation.

In nearly any community one can stir up an argument instantaneously on the question of whether or not board members should be required to have a college degree, or at least a high school diploma. It has been advocated at times that an intelligence test be required of candidates. In most states the only qualification for candidacy is to establish proof of being a voter of the district. This means that all candidates must be at least twenty-one years of age, but Kentucky specifies that board candidates must be twenty-four years old, while Wilmington, Delaware, and a few districts in Indiana and Missouri specify thirty years of age. Three states require that board members be taxpayers, and Arizona insists that they have a child in school. Idaho requires that a board member either be a taxpayer or have a child under twenty-one.

Only eleven states have any requirements for board members insofar as their education is concerned, and those are not exacting. Kentucky requires completion of an eighth grade education or equivalent for board membership, while the other ten states demand that members be "able to read and write," or have a "fair elementary education," or a "practical education."

Actually the debate over the desirability of insisting upon educational requirements for board members is more pedagogical than valuable. Most communities have difficulty arousing interest among leading citizens in becoming candidates for the board unless there is a major issue at hand. Persons who would make good board members generally have to be coaxed.

Relationship of Superintendent to Board

Under modern concepts of public school administration the most important single responsibility with which a board of education is charged is the appointment of a superintendent. It is somewhat ironic, therefore, that the greatest amount of friction between a board and its superintendent stems from the failure of either one to understand, or abide by, their respective jurisdictions. It seems logical to conclude, both from an interpretation of the intent of the law and from common sense, that a board was created expressly to see to it that provisions were made for the education of the children in each district and to assume responsibility for governing the institutions and personnel necessary for that purpose. Except in early history when the personnel involved, both pupils and teachers, were numerically few, and when the goals for a school were uncomplicated, it has rarely been expected that the citizens elected to provide the educational system would also be counted on to operate the technical aspects of education. That members of the early school committees actually did supervise and teach, and sometimes financed school operations in their territories, testifies to the simplicity of educational procedures of that day. Board members today do not profess to a knowledge of school law, finance, methods of teaching, or of how children learn; although many will disagree with professional reasoning, and some few will claim greater knowledge about a given situation than the professional technician.

The principle of legislative (board of education) and executive (superintendent) operation is commonly accepted today as the only prudent way to conduct this communal but technical activity known as public education. Conflict appears immediately whenever either function invades the other's jurisdiction, as happens far too often both ways. Admittedly, it becomes difficult to determine at times whether a given task is more executive than legislative. The best way to minimize the confusion or the deliberate trespassing is to spell out in as much detail as possible the exclusive duties of each party.

One of the first tasks of the superintendent on a new job is to see to it that the board's and the superintendent's operational responsibilities are in writing. In fact, a good method of evaluating a prospective vacancy is to discover if the chore has already been accomplished. Where it hasn't been done, a candidate may get a clue as to why the previous superintendent resigned, particularly if it was under unfavorable circumstances. The candidate for a superintendency should have an understanding with the board before he accepts the post that policies will be agreed upon in writing as soon as possible.

For the superintendent who wants help in developing a list of respective duties, there are numerous pamphlets available from the professional administrative organizations, the state departments of education, and many city superintendents' offices. It should be pointed out that the listing of responsibilities should cover specifics as much as possible. There will still be areas of dispute, in which instances the superintendent will do well to let the board majority have its way if the issue cannot be resolved through amicable discussion.

It will be noted that the above advice used the word "majority." A superintendent generally encounters little combat with the majority. It is the independent, froward character who gives him his sleepless nights. The fellow who was elected to "get the superintendent," who has a one-track mind for his pet notion, who is a self-appointed authority on educational matters, who represents a specific interest in the community however fribble it may be, who doesn't like the other board members anyhow, or who regards the gaining of a point with greater significance than the welfare of the school system; these are the filibusters to educational progress.

Included somewhere in this list, at least according to the off-the-record comments of board members and superintendents, is the feminine board member. The trend toward having at least one woman represented on a board of education, as well as on other elective bodies and in public offices, is definite around the nation, a further refinement of Susan Anthony's hustling for woman suffrage. Women do bring another point of view to educational decisions, a fact which promises hope for progress since mothers generally take more interest in school matters than husbands do. Moreover, the records reveal some outstanding contributions and service by lady board members. As one reckless superintendent put it, however, who for obvious reasons must remain anonymous until retirement, "I believe in wide representation on the board of education, but not to the extent of female temperament."

With all the progress in obtaining equal rights between the sexes, in the development of wonder drugs, and with all the exceptions to the rule, little has been accomplished in equalizing emotions or patterns of thinking. The patience of male board members for the woman's obsessions with seeming inconsequentials, and her inability to cope with financial, legal, and maintenance problems, and the female's scorn of the male's benign indulgence of her ideas and bewilderment frequently lead to split boards. More often than not, the split vote results more from mutual disrespect than from conflict of objectives.

The superintendent's position is an uneasy one in this situation. Until he has tried a few times, he will probably remain so naïve as to think that he can resolve the differences and create a harmonious family. Soon he rediscovers a truth no younger than the Garden of Eden, that no volume of psychology, philosophy, or technical know-how enables the male mind to comprehend that of the female. When the splits unfold, he will have both sides approaching him independently to sell a point of view. He can't afford to alienate either. Recommended courses of action are to be fair and consistent with all divergences of opinion, try to avoid public displays of hostility by controlling what goes onto the agenda, remember where the majority is when the chips are down, and occasionally send the female member a dozen long-stemmed roses.

There is no intended implication here that the board should be a rubber stamp for the superintendent. Independent thought among the members on any legislative body is one of the fortunate and puissant attributes of a self-governing people, and it should be encouraged. The misanthropic board member may actually be an asset. It has been said that "Every superintendent should have one painful heel on the board; it keeps him on his toes." There is merit in this attitude—up to the point where whimsy or caprice interferes with objective thinking on matters of public policy and of the education of children. Some comfort may be found in the realization that the harm generated by antagonistic, uncooperative, selfish, and quarreling board action is always short-lived. Sooner or later the strength of public election will straighten out any serious miscarriage of authority.

SUPERINTENDENT-BOARD CONFLICTS STEM FROM DIVERGENT BACKGROUNDS

Another apparently irreconcilable conflict in superintendent-board relationships is caused by divergent backgrounds of persons involved whose minds are so sharply conditioned by that background as to impede a facile meeting of viewpoints. The superintendent's customary environment of scholarship, ethics, philosophy, and culture must seek common highways with the farmer, the banker, the doctor, the laborite, the salesman, the furniture dealer, the housewife, the grocer, the engineer, the investment broker, the minister, and the harbor pilot. Each one may be an expert in his field, but as board members they are united to sit in judgment on another expert's advice in a field where they qualify only as apprentices. Regardless of experience, every adult has concepts on education which may mesh with the superintendent's in some respects but seldom in all. Yet the superintendent is expected to blend these opposing philosophies to improve the learning of youth.

CONFLICT BETWEEN THE EDUCATOR AND THE BUSINESSMAN

One of the more common barriers to a meeting of minds between the legislative and executive functions appears in the opposing attitudes of the superintendent and the businessman board member. Actually, the divergence should not be as frequent as it is, for each utilizes the knowledge and techniques of the other in everyday operations of their respective affairs. That they line up on opposite sides of an issue so consistently can often be attributed to reciprocal suspicion rather than true differences. Nevertheless, accusations and counter-accusations are heard, some of which are stimulated by patterns of habit.

The author has encountered an industrialist board member who insisted that teachers be placed on a check-in and check-out basis because he handles his employees that way. He could not understand that this procedure more often than not begets less service from teachers who are accustomed to disregarding scheduled quitting times in order to get a job done. Another industrialist board member wanted teachers rated for quality as he evaluated a product coming off the assembly line. Despite repeated discussions, he could not distinguish between the intangible teaching-learning process and a manufacturing process involving tools and machines.

Another argued for the twelve-months school year on the basis of economical usage of school facilities, completely overlooking the desires of parents as well as the peculiar service rendered by many of the community's facilities in addition to school buildings. He could not see the analogy in a hypothetical requirement that movie houses and cocktail lounges must remain open twenty-four hours a day.

Another businessman board member couldn't understand why the superintendent declined a vendor's offer of a week's free trip to Canada. "We do it all the time at our office," he asserted. Still another board member was ruffled when the superintendent wouldn't let him take home some of the federal surplus cheese which had been furnished to the school cafeteria.

The point is not being made, or even intended, that superintendents are always scrupulous and businessmen are not. There are enough examples of the opposite to contradict the idea. These instances are mentioned to illustrate the seemingly impossible task of reconciling the divergence of habits and backgrounds.

PROGRESS TOWARD REMOVING
SUPERINTENDENT-BOARD CONFLICTS

Fortunately, there have been some very definite and hopeful developments in recent years to overcome the blockades. More and more literature is appearing to make it easier for a layman to become oriented into educational objectives and *modus operandi. The American School Board Journal,* a widely circulated monthly periodical, is leveled toward this objective alone. Universities are assisting by sponsoring workshops for board members, some geared to helping the newly elected board member learn more about his responsibilities. Regional, state, and national organizations of school board members have spread with such rapidity in very recent years that the National School Boards Association sometimes conducts its annual meeting jointly with the American Association of School Administrators.

It is safe to claim that the baffles between educators' and laymen's thinking are being razed with considerable success. The job need not be left up to literature and meetings, however. More progress can be made by the superintendent when he is working directly with his board. Even if laymen can never fully comprehend the strange philosophy of a superintendent, they can work harmoniously if the superintendent will merely win their confidence in his ability and judgment. He can also help the process by trying assiduously to understand laymen's points of view. They, too, have worthwhile thoughts.

Guiding Board Action

Even though the superintendent is the hired hand of the board members, he is expected to direct their decisions and activity. This is not a miscarriage of intent, but merely the way it has to be. Laymen have their own individual livelihoods to earn, and they must rely upon the hired technician to bring matters to their attention for consideration and decision. Since a good board is holding the superintendent responsible for managing and improving the educational program, he must have an over-all objective toward which he is trying to move, and the board must be steered in that same direction.

In order to guide the action of five varying points of view, the superintendent needs more than technical knowledge about education. If he is to "plane the board" down to a smoothly operating team, he must also be equipped with a magician's hat of psychological techniques. Some professional writers might refer to this ability as executive skill or administrative leadership. Under any nomenclature, the superintendent is merely sizing up people and situations in order to pull out the right technique to accomplish an objective. An understanding of human nature is the basis for success in this operation.

For example, he must realize that no one enjoys being embarrassed, especially by ignorance. Therefore, he should deliver no surprise packages at a public board meeting. A superintendent should have an understanding with his board members that he will never surprise them at a meeting with an issue of importance—and vice versa. Consequently, items needing discussion and decision are known by all concerned long before the meeting. Some matters can be handled by telephone, others by a letter or a copy of the agenda being mailed to board members in advance of the meeting; still others may be discussed informally several months before being brought to vote at a public session.

ARE CLOSED MEETINGS EVER PERMISSIBLE?

Keeping board members informed of issues before they vote introduces the controversial consideration of closed, or caucus, or executive sessions, or informal meetings of the board and superintendent. The practice is frowned upon by the public in general and by news reporters in specific. They contend that public education is public business and that there can be no secrets. Some state laws even forbid cloakroom sessions; all states outlaw official action at closed meetings, as it should be.

However, responsible reporters will admit that certain issues should not be discussed publicly, such as the consideration of a possible building site before negotiations are consummated; expulsion of a pupil; or the evaluation of a teacher for re-employment. Superintendents and boards have as much responsibility for preserving the inviolability of some of their discussions as the doctor has for protecting the confidences of his patients. As undesirable and repulsive as it is to ethical superintendents, there are even times that some concealments can be shared with only part of the board membership.

IMPORTANCE OF TIMING IN PRESENTING ISSUES FOR VOTE

A keen sense of timing in dealing with board members is almost as important as what they think about an issue for winning its approval. Every experienced superintendent can recite instances when he came to the meeting loaded with arguments in favor of a given proposition only to have the board pass the recommendation without question; other times the members will discuss at length a picayune item for which the superintendent has made no preparation. He can learn to know the nature and urges of various board members, but he cannot always predict moods.

However, he must be alert to the temperaments of the individuals as well as those of the community. The announcement of a forthcoming bond issue will meet with favor at one time of the year while it may spark a township holocaust at others. The same may be said for the introduction of a sex hygiene course, the appointment of an assistant superintendent, a salary increase for teachers, the withdrawal from an interscholastic athletic league, or any other major item—and even sometimes a minor matter.

Another effective timing technique is to present an issue that threatens to arouse unfavorable reaction at the same meeting where one or more issues that promise favorable reaction are presented. Or one can unleash the unfavorable issue right after some event has occurred that created a good feeling in the community. There should have been at least one year's build-up of public information before announcing a proposed increased tax measure. Still another version of this technique is to release an unpleasant matter when some more important happening is attracting public attention. A smart general always picks his battlefield and time for attack if at all possible.

AVOIDING SPLIT VOTING

The strategist superintendent never presents an important issue to the board for vote until he knows its outcome in advance. If possible, he will wait until all members are in favor of the point, or at least be assured of a majority approval. He may send up a trial balloon to test the sentiment. He will try to avoid split voting since superintendents ordinarily concur in the desirability of unanimity in the board's voting. Communities can be cited that have never turned down a school tax measure where the board has a pattern of consistent unanimous voting.

There is no question that a united front among board members, and between board and superintendent, generates confidence within the school district. However, there are communities whose citizens are so accustomed to quarreling factions and to public airing of gripes that they look with suspicion upon unanimous opinions. The superintendent needs to know his community in this regard, too, but he should always try to keep educational debates above the level of those conducted by some politically elected bodies.

There is another psychological factor present in split voting. No one, save those rugged souls who enjoy martyrdom, finds pleasure in being wrong. Whenever there is a split vote among an uneven number of persons, someone has to become a minority, wrong in the eyes of the majority and possibly the community. By avoiding split voting the superintendent is merely helping people save face.

THE SUPERINTENDENT SHOULD RETREAT OCCASIONALLY

If the superintendent fails to anticipate accurately the outcome of the vote, or if he detects signs of misfires during the discussion, his vanity should not prevent his withdrawing the recommendation for "further study." One master tactician on this approach always made it a point to visit the dissenting members before the next meeting and attempt to sell the idea on an individual basis.

A related bit of advice for the superintendent is to the effect that he should never become so committed to an issue that he can't withdraw. This can happen by pursuing a goal without proper clearance with the board. It does not mean that a superintendent should never take a stand. On practically every assignment there will come a time when he must go to the point of laying his job on the line for a principle or issue. This can be risky business, and perhaps professionally fatal, but the superintendent without at least a drop of sporting blood is not going to accomplish much for education anyhow.

GIVE THE BOARD CREDIT FOR SUCCESSES

Still another psychological technique is obviously meritorious in all human relationships but is neglected far too often, by superintendents as well as by other executives. The superintendent should credit the board for a particularly favorable action regardless of whether it was his idea or theirs. Board members constitute the silo for so many of the community's thistles that they need all the clover the superintendent can sow. Male and female egos are alike in this respect. Society's conditioning of the male species has trained him to make light of flattery, but he loves it, and needs it, as much as a woman does. The superintendent will get more local publicity than he wants anyhow, so he should strew all the possible rose petals in the board members' paths.

WHAT DOES A BOARD MEMBER'S VOTE MEAN?

In guiding board action the superintendent will sooner or later hear a lively and philosophical debate among conscientious members as to what their vote means. RESOLVED: That a board of education member should vote according to what he thinks the majority of citizens desire, rather than in terms of what he thinks is best for the school system in the light of his intimate knowledge on the subject which is not normally available to citizens.

A magnanimous person elected to the board will arrive on the scene with the objective of rendering decisions compatible with what people want. This is morally correct. Eventually, however, he comes to realize that with the exception of items mentioned in his campaign platform, if any, he doesn't know what the majority of citizens desire. All he is likely to hear will come from intimate acquaintances, or from vocal, steamed-up, and immediately perturbed minorities which can be grossly misleading. Moreover, there is no certain way of discovering majority wishes unless the matter is put to public vote. Obviously, this is not practical for the great number of important matters upon which he must make a decision and vote. He also discovers that the mass of citizens, most of whom are apathetic about schools, are not equipped with the facts as he is—even with a good public relations program.

After he has gone through this line of reasoning, he is ready to accept the fact that when a person is elected to public office the people have in effect said to him, "We have confidence in your ability to make decisions for our welfare. You represent us, but it is up to you to arrive at your own decisions. If we don't like your decisions, we'll let you know about it at the next election." Every board member must come to this conclusion for himself, but the superintendent can hasten the process if he stimulates opportunity for the reasoning to get under way early in the new board member's term of office.

This point presents another argument in favor of all board

members being elected at large rather than by area representation. Under the latter plan, a board member feels such an obligation to constituents that it interferes with his ability to think and vote in terms of what is best for the entire school system. Most board members are of such caliber that they rarely, if ever, favor their home school district on any issue. Generally, they lean over backward to the benefit of other districts just to avoid accusations that they are partial to their own.

SHOULD A SUPERINTENDENT EVER WITHHOLD INFORMATION FROM THE BOARD?

The point has already been made on the importance of keeping board members fully informed on all matters. The time comes to every superintendent when he wonders if he is justified in withholding certain information, or at least part of the story. Marriage counselors ofttimes suggest that family harmony will be served best if one partner does not know all of the other's sins.

Only the individual superintendent can answer this question for himself as he weighs relative values—of the issue, of the school system, and of his own future. However, the advice given to superintendents in this regard is not to get caught withholding information. Confidence, a most important ingredient for superintendency success, will certainly be destroyed.

The superintendent is exempted, of course, from sharing with the board the numerous personal confidences which come to him. In his position he must serve frequently as a big brother confidant to employees, parents, and pupils. He is under no more obligation to divulge these matters to board members than to any other citizen.

LOCATE THE POWERS WITHIN THE BOARD

In order to "sell" his program to the board, the superintendent must also know where the strengths lie. In any group of people there is invariably one person whose opinions weigh more heavily than that of others. It may be the most experi-

enced board member, or the wealthiest member, the most
highly educated, or the most persuasive speaker. Some boards
are actually rubber stamps for the power. Whatever the reason
for, or the degree of, the strength, the superintendent will
further his ideas if he locates it early and conducts his strategy
accordingly. The center of power within a board may vary
according to the issue at hand. The real power may acquiesce
to the engineer board member on building construction matters,
to the doctor on health problems, or to the housewife on cultural matters. Generally, boards will not favor an issue if the
power is not convinced of its worth.

Occasionally there are two powers of opposite views within
a board, a condition which makes the superintendent's task
more thrilling. A more common phenomenon is the more or
less permanent factions or cliques. If the coalitions cannot be
harmonized, the superintendent is left with the challenge of
playing faction against faction. Split votes are inevitable under
such circumstances, leading to the unfortunate possibility of
split boards with 3-2 votes on practically every matter, each
faction's viewpoints spilling over into the community with
shameful disregard for the welfare of education. The superintendent will live longer if he moves to less resistant pastures,
but in the meantime he must do what he can for the benefit of
boys and girls who are the ones most seriously hurt by these
quarrels. Of course, he will string along with the majority as
much as possible, trying to play soft music when the differences
erupt. Time, or another election, is really the only panacea for
most of these outbreaks.

The Superintendent's Practical Allegiance
Is to the Board

In planning his strategy with the board, there is one further
important principle to remember, viz., that his ultimate allegiance is to the board. Several groups will be clamoring for his
loyalty—teachers, staff, PTA, taxpayers, church, sports fans,

and even his wife. While each group can make a valid case for its claim, and although the superintendent does have a responsibility to each, when the chips are down so far on controversial issues that he has to make a choice among them, he must remind himself of who hired him, who can fire him, and to whom the law holds him responsible. He is responsible *for* the teachers, staff, and pupils, but he is responsible only *to* the board.

Some superintendents parlay this fact beyond the call of duty. One superintendent of the author's acquaintance gave only a polite ear to his subordinates, colleagues, and to citizens, with a serious ear available only to the board, until channels of command were so broken the people got directly to the board with their complaints, resulting in a dismissal for the superintendent. A shrewd school head never gets caught in this jam. He resorts to his board responsibility only in those rare instances of irreconcilable problems.

In order to preclude misinterpretation of this point of view by the moral critic, it is probably necessary to put in writing that the author is not elevating allegiance to the board of education above allegiance to his own conscience and to the welfare of education. Limits to his obligations to the board are recognized.

Ethics in Superintendent-Board Relationships

If superintendents would pay serious attention to the suggestions in this section, they might have less need for those in the preceding paragraphs. Since not all do, and since a superintendent cannot be held responsible for the people elected to board membership, all of the suggestions probably have value.

One of the first important lessons for the superintendent to learn in practical ethics is that *board elections are off limits to him*. It also applies to election of officers within the board. This is an ethical point for the reason that the intent of public education laws was to enable citizens of a community to retain jurisdiction over their schools through the process of elective representation. It is an expedient point for the reason that the candidate for whom the superintendent is stumping may not always win.

Some superintendents will disagree on this advice. Some have been heard to boast that no one is ever elected to their boards who isn't endorsed, even hand-picked, by the superintendent. In the writer's opinion, this constitutes a flagrant violation of the state constitutional provisions for governing public schools, as well as of the principle of free elections—a concept which some teachers are trying to instill in children's minds. A superintendent who is guilty of trying to control board elections will learn dramatically about the foolhardiness of his actions when his candidates are defeated.

It is common practice for citizens who have confidence in their superintendent and who are considering the promotion of a candidate to discuss the situation with the superintendent. This can be an embarrassing predicament if the superintendent favors the re-election of present members. It need be no embarrassment at all, and can even be a means of developing respect among opponents, if he merely replies that he takes no part in board elections. He should not even sign a candidate's petition. The most he dares to risk is the role of a distant background counselor.

With the exceptions noted in a previous section, *the superintendent cannot play favorites with board members*. He should not entertain one without the others. He cannot share confidences with one and not the others. Since it is unlikely that he and his family can become intimate friends with all board members and their families, he should avoid intimacies with one. To do otherwise is not only unethical, but again, it isn't smart. Sooner or later the others will find out. Of course, he cannot prevent overtures from board members to close friendship or to share confidences. All he can do is refrain from initiating them.

Regardless of how many times a board overrules the superintendent, or of what balmy decisions the board makes, *once the vote is cast it becomes the decision of both the board and the superintendent.* The ethical, or astute, superintendent does not register public blame, does not pass the buck to them even if he disagrees with the decision, nor does he ever point to a particular member who might have blocked his recommendation. In the privacy of the board, or even in open discussion, there can be as much give and take as desired, but once the decision is made, it is *our* decision, not "mine" or "theirs."

It is essential that the superintendent be consistent in his views, statements, and actions. Although he needs to be sufficiently pragmatic to accept new evidence and change his mind if the facts make it logical, he cannot waver with the verbal winds. While this advice is applicable to other than ethical principles, it is included here as a matter of building good relations with the board. The author has observed a superintendent who was so adept with verbiage that he could start on one side of an issue but, if the powers seemed to be blowing the other way, tactfully change to the opposite side with equally strong arguments, and with the board members scarcely detecting the switch. This pleases both sides temporarily, and a superintendent can get away with it a few times; but eventually the impressions of vacillation and double cross will become stronger in the mind of a board member than does the momentary satisfaction of having the superintendent agree with him.

The warning, characteristic to the major emphasis of this book, is repeated here. No two boards operate precisely alike, any more than do two superintendents, two teachers, or two communities. A new superintendent must feel his way along with a board until he understands the idiosyncrasies of its members. Nevertheless, boards are composed of people who, though individualistic, demonstrate common reactions characteristic of the human species. Therefore, the principles suggested herein are those that appeal more to the generalities of people than to their exceptions.

chapter four

A Faculty for Administering

The superintendent with the happy faculty for keeping his faculty happy is destined for a successful career!

The teaching corps constitutes the most important element of the entire educational scheme, excepting the pupils, of course. They are the key to good learning, to the reputation of the school system, and to the success which a superintendent might attain. The effectiveness of teachers makes the superintendent look good or bad. The teaching staff also causes the superintendent most of his headaches, not just because of his struggles these days to find enough good ones, but because of his fagging efforts to keep them satisfied.

Mid-twentieth century has witnessed several changes which have aggravated the superintendent's task of maintaining a contented teaching staff: changes in society, economics, public attitudes, and in education itself.

All the dissatisfaction among teachers has not sprouted from inadequate salaries, but since that is the first cause that would come to many minds, it will be given priority here in citing the factors which contribute to low morale. Educators and civic-minded citizens can take pride in the advancements they have brought about in the past twenty-five years to improve teacher income. That period has seen the average annual salary paid to teachers practically double. And still the increase has not kept pace with the soaring cost of living during the same period, or with the ascent of income of other breadwinners—of wage earners as well as that of some other professionals. Public employees, office workers, and those engaged in other service occupations have actually suffered a declining net income during the prosperity era from 1940 to the present. Consequently, many teachers, especially men with dependents, have become increasingly dissatisfied with their economic plight, frequently aiming their criticism in the direction of the administration for not getting them more money.

Concomitant with this dilemma has been the growing shortage of teachers. The upward spurt of school enrollments during the post-World War II period, unparalleled in American history, has exhausted the supply of qualified teachers. Preparing teachers from the small pool of depression babies when the birth rate was at a low ebb for a sudden expansion of school enrollments has posed an impossible goal. This tremendous demand for their services has led some teachers to take advantage of a new status of independence, knowing that if they're not treated right in one school system they can go somewhere else and get a better job.

Within the profession there has been another development to cause increased difficulty in administering a faculty. During the past quarter century the hope that teachers would be protected from arbitrary, dogmatic, and whimsical dismissals has been generally realized in most states. In the pendulum reaction against this injustice, strict tenure laws have been enacted which make it virtually impossible to remove a teacher from the profession. In many states and communities the superintendent is left with the choice of tolerating inept teachers or taking the case to court with the accompanying embarrassment to everyone concerned, including the school system. While the vast majority of teachers perform conscientiously and capably, some weaklings press their advantage with their "unilateral" contracts to hasten the administrator's ulcers.

Considerable unrest among the teaching staff has been generated also by an incessant criticism of education since World War II. While it is human to resent criticism, few educators object to honest protests designed to improve the situation. As a class, educators are as analytical, self-critical, and desirous of self-improvement as any group of people. It is disturbing, however, to be attacked without knowing the real motive behind it. Evidence appears from time to time that the accusations originate from cranks, from reformers with a pet educational idea, from citizens who are more interested in private schools, from some vested interests, from groups devoted to reducing taxes, and from subversive elements seeking to destroy American faith in their public schools. Despite the evidence, it has been almost impossible to pinpoint the source or the real motive for the criticism. Underpaid teachers, frequently struggling in crowded classrooms with inadequate teaching materials, have been compelled to take time from their heavy schedules for trying to justify to a questioning public why they're doing what they're doing. Such a staff can become understandably restless.

The teacher's load has been magnified by an increasing lay expectation from their public schools. There is probably no teacher alive today who can remember when he was expected merely to teach subject matter. Older teachers can recall, however, how much has been added to their burden during their lifetimes. Without listing the various "extracurricular" activities in which the schools have become engaged in the name of developing the "whole person," every classroom teacher is expected to handle the character development of pupils, to help them plan life careers, to teach grooming and manners, to look after their health needs, and to make untold reports on what the child is doing, in fact what the teacher is doing. All of this frustrating addition to what was formerly a clear-cut obligation to perform a limited task has contributed to the teacher's dissatisfaction.

The courts have had a hand in making teachers nervous, too. There was a day when a teacher stood *in loco parentis* in dealing with students. They were extended the same authority in disciplining a child as the child's own parent, and the same understanding in case of occasional misjudgment. Recently the courts have been implying that a teacher is not permitted to make a mistake, and if she does, she is liable for prosecution.

Syndicated psychologists have made their contribution to the tension of the teacher by planting in the minds of parents that a child's total personality could be thwarted by punishment. Hence, by proving again that a little learning can be dangerous, the huckster psychologists have helped to create parents who rave or sue when a hand is laid on Johnny. These same parents, and some others, no longer support the teacher in handling these children. None of these conditions make the superintendent's job any easier in trying to keep teachers happy.

DISSATISFACTIONS FROM INDIVIDUAL DIFFERENCES

There can be added to these new contributions to making teachers unhappy the ever-present factor of individual differences which exist within any set of faculty members. For the past quarter century educational philosophy has been evolving to the point that today there are representatives on nearly every staff of what is commonly termed the "new" and the "old" in educational objectives which frequently erupt into bitterness.

Then there are the interdepartmental feuds, the suspicions and jealousies that exist between elementary and high school teachers, between the highly trained and barely trained teachers, the academic minded and the extracurricular minded, the men and the women, plus the personal animosities that develop among people who are linked by occupation over the years.

These are the obstacles that make the task of keeping a family happy and working harmoniously toward common ends extremely foreboding. And yet this is the responsibility of the superintendent. The first essential of command is to look after the needs of the troops. Let us see how the modern superintendent meets this challenge.

EVERY SUPERINTENDENT
FAILS ON TWO COUNTS

The superintendent will be ready to tackle the job of keeping his professional family happy if he makes two concessions from the outset. One, he can't possibly please every member of the staff. Two, no single technique or approach will satisfy all teachers.

The preceding section explains why every superintendent fails in these two respects—individual differences. They are as real among teachers as within any other group of persons. The superintendent is doomed for premature frustration if he entertains illusions about achieving a 100 per cent contented staff, or if he thinks he knows a technique that will work with all of the faculty. As soon as he reconciles himself to these failures, he is ready to commence licking the problem of staff morale.

The Common Wants of Teachers

The challenge of successful administration of a faculty is not as far beyond achievement as the introduction to this chapter would suggest. Teachers are not much different from any other professional group. A breezy book recently appeared on the market under the title, *A Teacher Is a Person,*[1] a revolutionary thought to some people. If this theme can be accepted, keeping teachers satisfied with their work is primarily a matter of treating them as any normal, educated person would wish to be dealt with as an employee.

Administering a faculty is simply the process of leading and guiding teachers toward the accomplishment of the educational purposes which the body is expected to pursue. Such administration includes, of course, clerical and routine executive service also; but this aspect is a part of all types of administration and has been treated adequately in other volumes. A funda-

[1] Wilson, Charles H. *A Teacher Is a Person,* Henry Holt & Co., New York, 1956.

mental step in the process of leading and guiding people is inducing their harmonious, cooperative effort. In order to achieve this type of cooperative effort there must be good will established first. Good will is based on the satisfaction of desires. By this syllogistic reasoning, therefore, administering a faculty is satisfying their common desires.

If one were to survey a faculty of a hundred teachers as to what they want at the moment, their answers would probably extend to more than five hundred different items. However, if the pollster requested that the staff indicate their basic expectations from their teaching experience, the list would dwindle to a few items. Various attempts have been made to determine these fundamental expectations of teachers, most of which can be summarized under thirteen headings. Many of these are similar to the wants of any employee. A few are peculiar to the teaching profession. Only four have even remote relationship to money; therefore, at least nine are within the reach of a superintendent in the poorest school district.

COMMON WANT—OPPORTUNITY TO SHARE IN GENERAL DECISIONS

The facet of democratic administration that involves shared decision-making is an often confused and misconstrued aphorism. Everyone believes in it but no two people see the same shades to its meaning. The autocratically inclined administrator parcels out insignificant tidbits for the staff to chew over. The eager democratic devotee would conduct a teacher poll on every decision to include the selection of grass seed for the school lawn. Again, there is the judicious inbetween that is really being sought by teachers and modern administrators.

A sensible concept of decision-making within an educational organization involves a process whereby those persons cooperate in the arriving at a decision or policy which has major significance for their professional activities and upon which they can be reasonably expected to have adequate information for sound judgment. This definition removes much of the flimflam surrounding the process. Such a definition also might include in the process students, parents, laymen of the community, or specialists on a given problem.

There are mutual advantages in the process of arriving at decisions jointly. It is compatible with the American individualistic philosophy and psychology whereby people accept a plan more readily if they have shared in its formation. It then becomes "my" plan, which is always a good one. The process is also amicable with the American feeling of self-dependence and self-responsibility. Hearty Americans resent any semblance of dominance. It is a common goal in our way of life to seek the situation in which one doesn't have to be beholden to anyone. Sharing in the decisions of one's working world contributes to the realization of that goal. Furthermore, the process frequently has merit for the administrator in that he gets good ideas which might not have otherwise occurred to him.

There are also some drawbacks to the joint decision-making process. It is a slow operation. It demands limitless patience on the part of an administrator who knows the right answer but must wait on the group to go through the same thinking process to arrive at the same answer.

Some teachers don't want to be bothered with the technique. They live in their classroom environment, conscientiously doing a good job, and are annoyed with committee meetings called to make a decision, even though it may affect their welfare or teaching situation. There is also the type of teacher who prefers to have decisions made for him. He, too, may be doing an excellent teaching job but actually prefers following whatever plan is laid out for him even if it is not to his liking. Then, there are some teachers who are incapable of participating in a give-and-take discussion and of contributing any worthwhile thoughts. Some of these want to join in anyhow.

Also, there are certain areas of educational activity which for various reasons cannot or should not be submitted for communal decision. For example, a board of education is held responsible by law for deciding specified issues. Also, the board is responsible to the people who elected the members to represent them in managing school affairs. Some of these matters may be delegated by the board to the superintendent, but to no other employee. The board, or the superintendent, may solicit the opinions of teachers on the problem, but the decision must be made by the executive or legislative agents of the public.

There are, of course, too many decisions that must be made by the superintendent to invite group participation on all of them. No board of education, or community, or teaching staff for that matter, would tolerate the inefficiency that would result from joint decisions on all educational concerns. Many problems are of such individualistic or insignificant nature that common sense precludes the practicability of submitting them to the joint decision of any representative faculty group.

It is also a fact, though not always admitted by teachers, that they are not as well prepared to contribute to some decisions as the superintendent is. If this were not so, all the administrative training offered by universities and the accumulation of administrative wisdom over the years would be of no value. Moreover, few teachers, if any, are in a position to view a school system in as comprehensive a manner as a superintendent is. In short, if the superintendent is not more capable than teachers of rendering sound judgment on certain school matters, even some affecting the well-being and classroom situation of teachers, the taxpayers are paying out a heap of money for a superintendent without enjoying due returns.

Types of decisions in which it can be reasonably expected that teachers can make a worthwhile contribution and can have a professional, if not a legal, right to share in the decision are selection of textbooks and other teaching materials, the building of a salary schedule, reorganizing a course of study, determining policies governing student conduct, planning an educational conference, determining equitable teaching loads, or the assignment of homework.

There can be no doubt about the legal right of the superintendent to make the final decision on all matters within a school system that do not require board of education decision. The modern superintendent, however, realizes the strength and morale potentialities of involving colleagues in many decisions in order to satisfy this common urge of teachers.

COMMON WANT—RESPECT BEFITTING A MEMBER OF THE TEACHING PROFESSION

Respect and recognition are basic urges of humanity, but the "respect befitting a member of the teaching profession" goes beyond average expectations. In the author's opinion it is not unreasonable or professionally selfish to claim that teachers are entitled to a status in the community hierarchy above that to which everyone is entitled as a human being, not because of who they are but because of what they do and what they represent.

There are several reasons why this assertion is justified. A teacher is an educated person, certainly an accomplishment worthy of some consideration in any society that regards wisdom as a virtue. A teacher renders service to the community and to family life. A teacher contributes more than the "average" citizen does to improving morality, instilling ambition, patriotism, and allegiance to those ideals which people generally regard as elements of the good life. A teacher substitutes for parents in many instances. A teacher is expected to represent qualities which most people hold high before their own children.

The teacher is also entitled to respect from the administrative level. It must be admitted that some principals and superintendents have developed an unwarranted status complex by virtue of their positions in a school organization. Others have sought to manage a staff through dominance rather than leadership. Under such circumstances the treatment received by teachers destroys self-respect and dignity. The first step, therefore, in providing proper respect for teachers is for the administrator to analyze his own attitude toward colleagues.

To assure that a teacher receives appropriate respect, however, is not completely within the control of the superintendent. He can achieve administrative-teacher respect through his personal relations with staff members and through the suggestions offered elsewhere in this chapter. But there remains the problem of teachers receiving due regard from citizens and pupils, the lack of veneration from the latter attributed somewhat to the attitude of the former.

Although there still obtains a degree of community awe toward teachers, it seems clear that the modern citizen's esteem for the teacher is less than that which was expressed for the nation's early teachers or for teachers in foreign countries. There can be several explanations advanced for this situation, most of which would involve opinion more than fact, but they are definitely not all related to teacher status as determined by their income level.

COMMON WANT—EFFICIENT SERVICING OF TEACHER NEEDS

This want is dealt with fully in Chapter 6, and necessitates here only the reminder that the superintendent has the responsibility for creating the type of organization which will give prompt but prudent service to the teachers' instructional and personnel needs. This is one of the common wants that entails money—enough to provide the personnel and organization to guarantee good servicing.

COMMON WANT—TIME TO TEACH

The plea for time to teach is heard with increasing crescendo as years pass. What teachers are seeking is a reduction of class interruptions and nonteaching duties.

Both have been growing in recent years, partially through no fault of the administration or school system. Much of the additional reporting instituted of late stems from state and federal requirements concomitant with their increased financial aid to schools. When people succeed in getting central governments to assume more and more responsibility for local education, they can expect the reporting to become more burdensome. The trend toward improved means of measurement of educational activity also beckons more statistics, written records, and reports.

Interruptions to classroom time are also on the increase, caused partially by the broadening concepts of education that involve pupils in experiences other than strictly academic ones. As laymen lean more heavily upon their public schools, they want more courses offered, they want more information distributed to homes through the pupils, or they want children to collect money for more worthy but time-consuming purposes.

Some superintendents, however, have unnecessarily contributed their share to the increased clerical duties of teachers. There is the statistical-minded executive who thrives on paper consumption, who keeps triplicate files of all deeds, dialogues, and didactics, who issues dozens of written directives, and who requires a never-ceasing string of reports from his teachers.

Ofttimes the objections from teachers that they have no time to teach is caused by their conventional notion of the nature of teaching which delimits the meaning of "teaching" to lecturing or conducting recitations, that all other teaching methods and all other school activities are boondoggle designed to interfere with "pure teaching." Today's instructors should recognize that teaching includes records, reports, discipline, cafeteria duty, dance chaperoning, educational trips, sports, music, health, and community service.

The criticism, sometimes valid and sometimes narrow, can be alleviated if the superintendent is of a mind to do so. He can, for example, try doing without a regular report which either he or the board has been expecting and see what happens. Administrators who have experimented with this technique claim that frequently a year elapses before anyone misses the report. If a school system can survive that long without having use for it, it probably isn't needed. Then try it with another record.

In order to reduce the interruptions to class time, the board of education should adopt strict regulations governing the releasing of students from class, announcements permitted over the public address system, absenteeism and tardiness, outsiders calling on teachers during class time, and similar activities that interrupt the teacher. There will inevitably be emergencies and exceptions to the regulations, but the administrator can help by keeping these to a minimum. He should examine emergencies when they arise to see if they really exist. And he has a continuing responsibility to train teachers to understand that teaching in a public school involves more than recitation.

COMMON WANT—FAIR TREATMENT

To be treated fairly is as important for the morale and mental health of adults as it is for pupils. It means as much to teachers as it does to personnel in any other organization.

This common want of teachers means that the superintendent can have no favorites among the staff; it means that he must avoid close individual friendships on the faculty; it means making no exceptions to the salary schedule once it is adopted, however deserving a teacher might be; it means developing a system of equitable teaching loads; it means honesty with all staff members and talking to them out of the same corner of the mouth as he does to the board of education or to the public; and it means pointing out teachers' weaknesses as well as their good qualities.

It is really not difficult to satisfy this want among teachers, and it requires no money. It does call for courage. Teachers respect firm, fair, and consistent treatment even if they don't always agree with the decisions made under this approach.

COMMON WANT—TO BE KEPT INFORMED

A chapter is devoted later on to the significance of keeping the community informed about public school matters. The need is as imperative for persons within the school system. Public relations conscious superintendents sometimes work assiduously at keeping their publics informed of school affairs to the extent they forget that the core of their enterprise functions more cooperatively if they, too, know what is going on, that no one enjoys working "in the dark," and that ignorance of over-all plans and objectives breeds insecurity and gossip.

Within the ranks of schoolteachers grinds what is perhaps the greatest rumor mill outside of the military services. Research sheds no light on the reason why rumors so frequently originate from one common source, but one can detect similarity between the teachers' rest room and the army latrine in this respect at least. Without facts, rumors are bound to spring up and spread, sometimes to the detriment of the administration and the school system. The superintendent can't stop all the rumors, but he can reduce them by a deliberate pattern of keeping staff members informed.

The problem becomes more severe as school systems increase in size. In contrast to the one-building system where teachers come in contact with the superintendent daily, the head of a city system must utilize more than one means of maintaining communication with the staff. The regular weekly bulletin that announces events, decisions, and contemplated plans helps. Except in the very large city systems, there should be several general faculty meetings during the year if for no better reason than to enable the staff to get "the word" directly from the top. Individual building meetings with the superintendent present form a still better way of keeping rapport with the faculty.

Various types of representative faculty organizations can be utilized for channeling information to and from the chief executive. These might be the building principals, advisory council, or departmental heads, or all three.

Summaries of important official board action might be circulated among the faculty if it is impractical for teachers to attend the meetings for one reason or another. There is no better way to alleviate staff suspicion about "secret" high level discussions than to invite faculty members to be present. Just as with the doubting Thomases of a community, dubious teachers generally won't bother to come to these meetings if they know they are welcome.

Many modern superintendents pursue the "open door" approach with faculty members, and even though the intent is honorable, it doesn't work well if the staff is sizable. There isn't enough time during the year for everyone to see the boss personally, and if a teacher makes the attempt only to find the administrator absent or busy for a period, she doesn't bother to try it again. Superintendents who boast that their door is always open to faculty members may think they are keeping lines of communication open but they seldom realize how distant they appear to the staff.

COMMON WANT—APPROPRIATE SUPERVISION

This document does not essay to be a dissertation on the philosophy and techniques of supervision—of which there are ample treatments. Just enough about supervision will be included here to serve the purpose of this chapter, namely, to suggest means of accomplishing the administrative job of keeping teachers happy though supervised.

Surprisingly, most teachers want supervision. They are flattered with the attention. It is the manner in which supervisors have sometimes gone about the task that has led to faculty resentment. Furthermore, practically all teachers need supervision, periodically at least. The best teacher in the school system needs to be checked on occasionally. Because of the human tendency to let up if a person thinks no one is interested in what he is doing, it becomes obligatory for an administrator to prod good teachers just by putting in an occasional appearance. That, and a pat on the back, is all that is required for this caliber of teacher.

Many teachers, and practically all at one time or another, need help and suggestions that an able supervisor can provide. For these three reasons, supervision is an essential phase of administrative responsibility.

Notwithstanding the protests of insecure teachers and of democratic professors of the radical variety, a good supervisory program involves actual classroom visitation. There have been allegations that unscheduled classroom checks by supervisors are undemocratic, unnerving, even unfair. Only those teachers who have something to hide actually subscribe seriously to this point of view. While there is a definite place for scheduled or called visits to classrooms, experienced supervisors know too well the show they sometimes are privileged to observe when the teacher knows in advance that the chief is coming. Supervisors have also smiled at the sudden switch in lessons shortly after they arrive in certain classrooms. Teachers should learn quickly that this response to the supervisor's appearance brings several return visits.

The author will never forget a clever and amusing ruse used by a high school teacher whom he visited early in his career. Student response in the class was lively. Hands were up for every question asked, and the correct answer came forth every time. He was not only impressed but fascinated. After half an hour of this vivacious recitation, the teacher and students burst out laughing almost simultaneously. The teacher then explained that he had a pact with his students. The rules provided that when a supervisor was in the room, only the students with their left hands in the air knew the answer to the teacher's questions.

For the benefit of staff morale, it can be underscored again that teachers are entitled to know the results of the supervisor's visit. This is part of the job of keeping teachers informed as well as of contributing to their need for self-respect and fair treatment. The post-visit conference is almost as important as the visit itself.

A further suggestion for the superintendent in this brief discourse on supervision. He will attain a good supervisory program as soon as he realizes that building principals must do most of the supervision. Few school systems will ever have enough money to afford the number of supervisors required to maintain the frequency of visits, evaluations, and conferences that are desirable. The superintendent will find it much more economical and effective to make provisions for the principal to be relieved of his clerical obligations and then train him to supervise intelligently. Evaluation of teachers is not accomplished by classroom visitations alone. Nor can one divorce teacher evaluation from the numerous other activities in which she is engaged around the building about which only the principal has knowledge daily.

COMMON WANT—FREEDOM FROM BOREDOM

Even though education is a changing process and involves mental activity, it is almost as easy for a teacher to become bored with her task as it is for persons engaged in other occupations. The rut can be just as deep, but the effect is more serious in that it influences the lives and minds of many children. Some teachers bore more easily than others; some actually enjoy monotony. In order to keep a happy faculty, the superintendent must devise means for keeping his teachers alive intellectually, physically, and emotionally.

One way to combat boredom among teachers is change— change of assignment, change of room, change in procedures from year to year, change in principal, and change in extra duties. Many teachers will resist the change. There are teachers known to have held onto the same classroom for thirty years who will cry at the suggestion of changing to another, even if it is a better room. A change in teaching assignment will bring forth vigorous objections by many teachers. When these cries are heard, the superintendent can be sure that the people are in the familiar rut and need a change. Almost without exception, such teachers are appreciative of the change within a short time after it has been consummated.

The need for relief from boredom adds support to the policy of promoting to higher positions from within the system whenever feasible. By the same token, demotions may act to stimulate a person who is coasting.

Varied faculty social affairs can help to provide emotional release and uplift. Challenging in-service training programs have stimulating effects. The money budgeted for sending teachers to conferences and visitations to other schools can be justified on these grounds alone.

The requirement of some schools for teachers to return to the university for additional training periodically in order to advance on the salary schedule has value for this purpose even if the person learns little he can use in the classroom— which is unlikely. Committee work and added responsibilities, though usually protested, can serve as a relief from boredom.

In effecting change for the purpose of avoiding boredom, the superintendent must demonstrate judgment in order to prevent undue confusion. Change for the sake of change can be overdone. In fact, there is enough meat for another book just in the psychology of change and how it may be accomplished successfully. Timing is of the essence. Many administrators have stubbed toes in their inability to sense the right climate for change, especially in the first year of an appointment—the period so vital to one's success. Changes are expected of a new administration, immediately and drastically if school conditions are poor, but slowly and moderately if the previous administration has left the schools in good shape. The newcomer might well capitalize on his predecessor's achievements by controlling his eagerness to improve matters for at least a year. To find the optimum course of action, the administrator must be sensitive to the emotional structure of individuals and to the pulse of the entire organization and community.

COMMON WANT—ADMINISTRATIVE UNDERSTANDING OF TEACHER PROBLEMS AND VIEWPOINTS

The accusation that administrators do not understand teachers' problems and viewpoints is commonly heard. The complaint is stimulated by several factors: the feeling of "aloneness" that ofttimes envelops teachers in larger school systems because of the distance that separates them from their administrators; individual wishes that have to be denied by the administrator; staff recommendations that must be reversed occasionally because of extenuating circumstances; and sometimes by administrators with confused allegiances who are guilty of slighting their staff obligations.

Generally, however, the accusation is distorted, for more often than not the situation is just the reverse—teachers fail to understand the problems and viewpoints of superintendents. The structure of a public school system, and the nature of the training for the various personnel components of education, make this failure inevitable. All administrators have been teachers and have pursued teacher-training programs, while very few teachers have had administrative experience or have even enrolled for a single administrative course in college. Moreover, teachers work in isolation to a degree, capably fulfilling the assignment that has been given them, but having no time or opportunity to view the school system in its entirety as a superintendent must do. While this situation will undoubtedly continue to obtain, superintendents can share their strategic outlook somewhat by doing a better job of keeping all staff members informed of problems and developments.

Some attempts have been made maliciously, if abortively, to widen the gap between administration and teaching by a small group of teachers who aspire to introduce labor unionism within the profession. In order to rationalize this irreconcilable coalescence, and having a need for a werewolf against which a rallying cry can be built, they have conjured up within the profession a separate entity labeled "management"—an ogre that must be intimidated and embarrassed. An administrator might accept these groups as merely another deterrent to his efforts toward providing the community with a good school system if it were not for the setbacks to the school's good will their antics sometimes effect. On occasion he must take time out to repair weaknesses within the profession and the community so that he can continue his objectives of gaining for the entire staff the ends which these organizations are presumably seeking.

The modern superintendent does demonstrate a keen understanding of what teachers need and want, of the problems a teacher faces from day to day, of the motives that prompt teachers to their actions, and he is far out in front in trying to provide for their needs.

COMMON WANT—SECURITY

The urge for security obtains in varying degrees among all persons, becoming more intense with age. Admittedly, some people enjoy the thrill of uncertainty, risk, and adventure, and nearly all youth are excited by the unknown, but maturity effects a sobriety that enhances the desire to live in reasonable assured comfort.

The security which teachers generally enjoy today has not always been a virtue of the trade. Older teachers can still remember the day when they were subject to the fickleness of the school administration or board of education, or to that of citizens who could readily exert sufficient pressure on either of the former to have a teacher removed from her position. Any person who works with parents' most priceless possession— their children—and furthermore, who excites youthful minds to probe the uncertain catacombs of ideas, is destined for suspicion and resentment. Such a person needs protection from the moods and whims of those who control his job. Future teachers could scarcely be persuaded to prepare for the field if there were not some means of protecting their investments in college degrees.

If the financial returns from the teacher's efforts were highly correlated with the extent of his required training, even closely approximating that of other professionals, the need for financial security would not be so great. Since that comparative correlation does not exist, and since the teacher enters a field with a fixed income ceiling, certainly he is entitled to some compensatory features, say a greater promise of security.

Today the financial and position security urge has been satisfied for most educators. Nearly every educational institution has its local or state retirement plans for old-age security. Protection from unreasonable loss of position has also been realized via the various tenure plans. Short term protection has been given teachers through the contractual feature of their employment. Additional security is available to most teachers by means of sick leave provisions, sickness and accident insurance policies sometimes provided by the employer, and leaves of absence for numerous reasons.

Security for any position, however, is not without disadvantages. Perhaps the most severe demerit in security provisions is their encouragement to complacency. While security is intended to free teachers from personal distractions so that they may concentrate on the task, it also tends to erode their drive to improve and advance. Although all people do not yield to the temptation, it is a human characteristic to "let down" when one is assured of his goal. The most aggravating feature of teacher security plans, both for the administrator and for good faculty members, is the protection extended to the weak as well as the strong. No one, except the weak, likes this aspect of tenure and retirement plans, but the weak do seem strong enough to prevent anything being done about it.

COMMON WANT—ADMINISTRATIVE SUPPORT

Still another common want among teachers is support from their administrators in the execution of their teaching responsibilities. A frequent reason for the complaint that administrative support is lacking results from the complications of semantics. "Administrative support" means different things to different people.

The administrator owes the teacher support in her classroom decisions, in her disciplining of students, in her relationships with the public and the board of education. Even when she is wrong in minor disputes, he should support her in the presence of the antagonist. In serious violations of policy, regulations, or good judgment, he may acknowledge teacher error in the presence of the pupil or outsider, but must try to soften the feeling. A tactful superintendent, mindful of a teacher's need to save face, might assume a share of the responsibility for the wrongdoing. However, he has an equal obligation to correct the teacher in privacy. In this way an administrator can normally maintain the teacher's respect and loyalty, but an unfair or extremely sensitive teacher will still accuse the administrator of not supporting her.

The cry of "no support" arises most frequently in disciplinary situations. A common practice in school buildings is for the teacher to send a misbehaving child to the office for punishment. Usually the teacher has exhausted her techniques for maintaining discipline and is calling for help from the principal or superintendent. She is at the end of her rope and emotionally upset, perhaps downright angry. The administrator may be in a different frame of mind upon receiving the pupil and can exercise calmer judgment in meting out the punishment. If, however, the sentence is anything less than what the teacher had in mind when she sent the pupil scurrying, she is convinced the administrator has let her down. She has not had her pound of flesh out of the student and receives "no administrative support." The executive can alleviate this difference of opinion if he develops an understanding with the faculty that when a teacher sends a pupil to the office for disciplinary purposes, she has said in effect, "I can't cope with this problem and absolve myself of responsibility for correcting it. It is now up to you, and I accept your decision."

Even under the atmosphere of democratic cooperation, the administrator must remember that he has the responsibility, established by the board of education's delegation of authority and sometimes by law, to appraise teachers, commend them, support them, criticize and censure them as the situation demands.

COMMON WANT—LIVABLE INCOME COMMENSURATE WITH TRAINING AND CONTRIBUTION

Everyone associated with schools directly or indirectly knows that teaching salaries are inadequate, but no one knows exactly what they ought to be, nor on what basis salaries ought to be determined. While the debating goes on, salaries of public school employees are predicated upon just two factors: what a community can be persuaded to pay and what other communities are paying. All other factors are picayune adjustments in an attempt to develop something equitable for the numerous categories of employees.

It is difficult to relate the value placed on a teacher's service to any other force operating within a community except the two factors mentioned. The value is related remotely, if at all, to the economic laws of supply and demand that affect income of other occupationals. Although school officials capitalize on the difficulty of getting teachers as a reason for increasing salaries, somehow the classes always have a body in the front of the room whether salaries are increased or not. Salaries are not related to the teachers' contribution to the welfare of the community, quite obviously. And certainly teaching salaries are not related to the extent of investment in preparation for the job.

If one should attempt to develop an equitable basis for the determination of teaching worth, certainly the two most prominent factors would be personal investment in preparation and contribution to humanity. It is doubtful, however, if these two aspects will ever receive the consideration they deserve because the public dictates the amounts to be paid. People have always resisted taxes and probably always will, and everyone endeavors to get the most value for the least expenditure. Moreover, the factor of training does not impress Johnny Public. He would pay doctors less if he could get away with it, or lawyers, or car dealers, or bakers. Citizens demand extensive training from their teachers but are not sufficiently impressed with it to pay much more in order to get it.

This line of reasoning makes the idea of teachers' revolting from their work appear justified. If parents once lost their public schools, they'd find the necessary funds in a hurry. There have been dozens of examples of a board of education, or a community, gladly paying more money to keep a good man when they fear they are about to lose him. As appealing as the idea of revolt might be, it will never happen. There are too many conscientious captains among the teaching ranks who would rather go down with the ship than let it sink.

There are other reasons, or excuses, that will prevent public school teaching salaries from being what they ought to be. Many employees in other fields look at the summer, Christmas, and spring vacations that schools observe and conclude that teachers are already overpaid. They see many teachers earning extra money in the summertime and look upon this practice as an opportunity for earning two incomes. Some people see only the relatively short hours that teachers are actually on the job and think that that's all there is to teaching. There is a substantial amount of resentment among feminine workers in other occupations who read about the higher salaries female teachers receive and forget about the preparation the teacher had to complete. It is true that the teaching profession offers the best opportunity of any vocation for masses of women to earn a comfortable salary. It is one of the poorest paid occupations for men, especially for the young men on the staff who are just getting started with a family and home.

The few bad apples on a faculty also seriously hurt the remainder of the staff. The bad apple here works the same as in the infamous barrel, spreading his disease throughout the community. Too many people, including board members, are inclined to think of the apple when they are deciding what a teacher ought to earn rather than concentrating upon the many good teachers.

It is common knowledge among experienced school superintendents that board members from lower income brackets frequently block better salaries for teachers. It is probably natural that anyone resents people who make more money than he does. A wealthy board member can be appealed to in behalf of the cause for better salaries and he will not experience any personal resentment if the increase is granted. To the mind of the low-income board members there is returning constantly the thought, "Why should a teacher make any more money than I do?"

Then there are the usual groups in any community who silently or openly resist any increased taxation for better public school teaching salaries: property owners of sizable proportion, supporters of private schools, adults with no children in school, and those who for one of a thousand reasons just don't like something about the schools.

When all of these opposing forces are considered, it is a wonder that salaries for public school educators have risen even to their present status. It is a tribute to the salesmanship of school administrators that they have been able to persuade citizens to do as much as they have. It emphasizes the point made elsewhere in this volume that the foremost responsibility of the superintendent is public relations.

COMMON WANT—OPPORTUNITY TO RELA.

Few laymen understand the pressure that teachers feel during a day with thirty suppressed packages of dynamite, or the fatigue they experience at the end of the day. Sometimes superintendents forget. On most days teachers just want to be left alone when their duty is officially ended.

In order to keep a faculty happy, the superintendent needs to exercise caution in scheduling after-school and evening meetings. He should also be conscious of the necessity for distributing extra assignments instead of overloading the willing and capable horses.

For some teachers, the administrator should deliberately plan opportunities for relaxation and diversification. Young and new teachers in the system desire recreational opportunities. For others, some provision should be made for cultural and intellectual diversions. In arranging such opportunities, the superintendent must guard against the appearance of paternalism and against fostering the feeling of obligation that teachers must participate. As has been said, most teachers just want to be left alone after school hours.

chapter five

Curriculum Carrousel

As much as a superintendent gropes singlehandedly through his daily obstacle course with no local source for counsel, there is one undertaking for which he has abundant offers of assistance—curriculum revision. He has more sidewalk superintendents for this project than do all the nation's construction engineers combined.

One superintendent reports that during his fifteen years of school administration it is doubtful if one week went by without his receiving at least one unsolicited suggestion for improvement of the curriculum. Working 50 weeks a year, that totals 750 additional learning units by which the education of boys and girls could have been enriched. "In some weeks business was even better," he adds. The central staff of another school system of 20,000 pupils once sought a scientific basis for rejecting suggestions for curriculum expansion. Research does not establish whether that year consituted a record, but the survey tallied exactly 126 requests for school children to participate in this or that education experience, in addition to the conglomeration to which pupils somehow had already adjusted.

Ideas for expanding the curriculum come from untold sources in a community, from wherever a group devoted to a specific interest believes the unwashed populace would be happier if they all shared the same interest, and that the best place to start washing is in the public schools. The Garden Club wants gardening taught in the schools, the Kiwanis Club wants to start a young Kiwanian Club, a church wants Bible study, local recruiting agents want military information disseminated, bankers want savings clubs started, hospitals want a course in nurses' training, engineers want a mathematics club launched, the League of Women Voters wants more political education, welfare agencies want a course in birth control, dance studios want classes in dancing, the Athletic Club wants more physical education, the Art Institute wants more art for art's sake, the Bricklayers' Local wants another apprenticeship class, *ad infinitum*. Even our federal government gets into the act as evidenced by its pushing the purchase of savings stamps among school pupils. No word yet from the distilleries.

The curriculum is tampered with enough by the professional tamperers—universities, practicing school personnel, and board of education members. Most of them are paid to tamper. They are best qualified insofar as they have educational knowledge and experience. While they are occasionally accused of promoting individual ideas or selfish interests, most of these persons are sincerely dedicated to improving the learning methods and opportunities. Their technical knowledge for this purpose is unsurpassed in our society, but they are sometimes prone to be too close to the problem for objectivity. They are not always tuned to public sentiment regarding education.

The superintendent will have a cupful of headaches in steering those groups through the pull of opposing philosophies toward a steady course in revising the learning program for the best needs of youth. It is merely a cupful compared with the ocean of hard knocks he will experience in coping with the unprofessional, volunteer curriculum revisers at large in any community. It is with this larger group, then, that this chapter will deal. There are five major classifications.

THE DOWN-THE-LINERS

The down-the-liners, referred to in pedagogical parlance as fundamentalists, predicate their desires to revise the curriculum on a concept of the educated man as being a scholar, and little else. In order to be a scholar one needs to be skilled only in what is commonly termed the fundamentals of learning —reading, calculating, composition, and spelling. Later on the fundamentals might include science and foreign languages. Everything else on the learning menu is merely dessert concocted by starry-eyed educators bent on socializing the community. They manage to gloss over the original premise of public education which sought to make it possible for all children to receive at public expense an opportunity to learn.

The down-the-liners may be classified further into two camps—the orthodox and reformed. The reformed, or liberals, would be willing for young people without sufficient gray matter for mastering the fundamentals to be trained at public expense in an institution known as a vocational high school. The orthodox would have these youths merely shunted aside. They don't bother to elaborate on what institution in our society is expected to look after the shunted—or what that cost might be.

Fundamentalists criticize these aspects of the school program: social studies, athletics and physical education, extracurricular activities, field trips, guidance program, vocational subjects, home economics, life adjustment courses, and all modern methods of teaching. They criticize, too, the lack of emphasis on fundamentals.

The blue blood fundamentalists are frequently joined by fringe bedfellows who score educators for failing to do right by their pet fundamental. To wit, there are the employers of stenographic personnel who can't spell, of factory workers who can't compute, of retail clerks who can't add, of engineers who can't compose readable reports, of soda jerks who don't want to work, of shipping clerks who can't read foreign languages, of carhops with undisciplined morals, of reporters who know little history, or of truck drivers who don't know how to drive safely. Wherever an employer uncovers a weakness in one of his youthful hired hands, he is disgusted not only with the hand but also with those who trained him. Add all these potential complainants together and one comes up with quite a bevy of critics who berate the curriculum designers for neglect of the fundamentals.

PROTAGONISTS FOR THE CORE CURRICULUM—ATHLETICS

Athletic boosters are the loudest curriculum revisers if not the most numerous. No phase of the school program in the average to medium-sized system causes more noise and unrest than do interscholastic sports. The extremists are not particularly concerned with revising the curriculum; they don't even care whether there is one. They are obsessed only with the core curriculum—athletics. The more moderate enthusiasts do not want to interfere with the education of children, which they concede is the big function of schools, but, well, they would just like to see the football team win more games.

One superintendent, upon reporting the first day on a new job, discovered his desk was thoroughly cleaned out with the exception of a few nervously chewed pencils and a 3 x 5 file card with this parody:

> Count that one day heavenly blest
> When no athletic problem is on this desk.

The meter was bad, the rhyme sufferable, but the content clear. It exaggerates the typical administrator's predicament only slightly.

Whatever superintendents do with the athletic program, they're bound to be chastised. If the high school loses many games, then the coach "has gotta go." If the curriculum revisers are good friends with the coach, then there is heard any or all of the following cries familiar to the experienced administrator:

"The superintendent is against athletics."

"Modern education discourages competition."

"The schedule is too tough."

"The feeder system from junior high and elementary is weak."

"More assistant coaches are needed."

"The principal should hold more pep sessions."

"The coach's teaching load is too heavy."

"Kids aren't what they used to be."

And de-emphasis!—that abhorrent word which strikes fear in the hearts of every sports lover but for which no one has an unambiguous definition.

On the other hand, a streak of victories will quiet most of the grandstand professionals; not all, but most. From other quarters is then heard: that

"The coaches are paid too much."

"Educational standards are slipping."

"The boys ought to play tougher opposition."

"Only a few students participate."

"High school sports should have more carry-over value."

Sooner or later there will be an investigation and a tightening of athletic regulations.

It is intriguing to analyze the reasons for the urge to produce strong high school athletic teams. Some advocates claim that winning teams are "good for business," and yet most stores are closed on the night of the games and no evidence has yet been uncovered of an industry locating within a town because of its high school athletic records. Others say that a rugged sports program stimulates the competitive spirit. There can be little argument on this point. The only question centers around the urgency for all the hullabaloo of a powerhouse athletic team to accomplish it when the schools already encourage the competitive spirit in a hundred other less spectacular ways. Competitive spirit is seldom keener than in a lively sixth-grade spell down or the competition among high school boys for the favor of a cute senior, but no stadium has ever been built or filled to witness either type of contest.

Still other rabid core enthusiasts argue that winning athletic teams generate a community spirit for better schools in

general. They leave unexplained the fact that in one small city
known widely for its championship football teams the school
board for years could not pass a bond issue to provide adequate classroom space.

In order to keep the learning program in balance, the superintendent needs to understand who it is in the community that
wants to tamper with the athletic curriculum. Who is responsible for permitting the dog-wagging sports tail to depart so
markedly from the original reason for a school's providing
opportunities for boys and girls to play games?

Certainly coaches aren't to be blamed for building themselves into such a frenzied state that they can't eat, can't tolerate their wives, and can't escape without resigning for a regular teaching position. The sports scribes, often accused of
glamorizing the athletic heroes and coaches, duck responsibility by answering that they write only what the public wants.

Any line of reasoning which the analyst pursues eventually
leads back to the public. Whether it is the public of a public
institution, or the alumni public of a private institution, there is
just one clear certainty—nothing remains in a school curriculum long which the public does not want. As will be demonstrated shortly, there may be confusion about who the public
is; nevertheless, the public does own the public schools.

MINUTEMEN CURRICULUM REVISERS

As certain as there are national tensions, there will be
groups bent on revising the curriculum so that tomorrow's
adults will not be tense. In periods of national tranquillity few
persons seem worried about what youth is learning. In wars,
depressions, inflations, crime waves, drought, political up-
heavals, and Hallowe'en alarming cries are heard about what
is going into the minds of children. The cries are followed by
investigating committees, textbook inquiries, loyalty oaths,
allegations, and an occasional discovery of a traitorous scalawag. There must be a cause found for all this lecherous skull-
duggery and, sooner or later, the finger turns to the one agency

that influences all youth, and, incidentally, costs a heap of money, the public schools. After sounding the depths of teachers' loyalty, the search proceeds to the teaching methods, textbooks, and the curriculum. American elementary and secondary school curriculums have been expanded substantially through these moments of tension.

Still another brand of fundamentalists sometimes joins the posse to attack the social studies, which rings like socialism in some ears, and clamors for a return to pure history, whatever that is. They stump for more history, more pledges of allegiance, more essays on Americanism, more study of the Constitution, and more trips to the state capitol—all of which absorbs so much of the school day as to crowd out other fundamentals of reading, figuring, and spelling.

If the superintendent is not on his toes, he will be caught in one of those "When did you stop beating your wife" vises. If he stands up to defend the staff and curriculum, he arouses suspicion about his own loyalty. If he permits the throwing out of textbooks, pulling reference books from the library shelves, and overhauling of the curriculum, he admits he has been lax in tending to the learning of the American heritage.

In these moments of excitement people seem to forget that the strong, but sometimes dormant, nationalistic attitude which grips most Americans has been developed largely in the public schools. Where else but in the American classroom did most people, youth and adults, acquire their understandings of American heritage, history, geography, and heroes; their knowledge of government, courts, flag, and Constitution; their familiarity with patriotic songs, pledge, and literature? Certainly, the homes or churches or any other institutions of society exercise little influence in developing patriotic knowledges and attitudes.

MORALISTA CURRICULUM REVISERS

Between national tensions the superintendent has years of relief from the patriotic curriculum revisers, but he is never free from the reformers who want to upgrade the nation's morals through the school curriculum. The news media are sufficiently filled with immoral conduct at all times to keep the pressure on educators continuous. Since most of the groups concerned with improving national morality have already abandoned hope for adults, they naturally turn to youth. The only facile way of getting at youth, again, is through the schools and their learning exercises.

This publication does not intend to probe the uncongeniality of parochial and public educational institutions or the denominational discords. It is concerned here only with the influences on the curriculum from religious and moral pressures. The revisers may want religious instruction during or near school time, instruction on the evils of cocktails and tobacco, Bible reading and prayer, elimination of square, round, or folk dancing in physical education classes, distribution of the Gideon Bible to pupils, or merely the addition of books and magazines to the school library.

PRIVATE INTEREST CURRICULUM REVISERS

This category of voluntary curriculum revisers is comprised primarily of the hundreds of commercial groups who visualize in public schools an opportunity for acquainting future consumers with the virtues of their respective products. There is no limit to the products, short of immoral ones, or to the resourcefulness of the revisers in making the educational opportunities available to boys and girls. Superintendents find it difficult to circumvent the offers when they are reminded that the vendors are taxpayers, which they usually are of some importance.

For years the common device used by these groups to get something added to the curriculum has been a contest, usually a poster or essay. As suggested earlier, if a school system took advantage of all the offers each year, the quantity of art and composition would be enlarged materially but the teacher would scarcely have an opportunity to touch on quality. Some of the prizes are so enticing that the superintendent can only hope the students never learn of the potential awards he denied them. There are enough trips to Washington and New York alone each year that, if participation were permitted and pupils were lucky, the teacher would have better attendance if she conducted her classes about halfway between, at say Atlantic City.

Many vendors in recent years have discovered the apathy with which superintendents look upon contests and have developed variations. The latest popular gimmick for getting a commercial point of view wedged into the curriculum is the educational comic book. Pupils do like comics, and they get a special delight when a study hall teacher snatches it from them only to discover it is an educational comic book. Some of the productions are top grade. Industry has done a commendable job in capitalizing on a natural desire toward the creation of a truly worthwhile visual aid. Most of the producers can't resist, of course, annexing somewhere a plug for the company. Since most school systems have a regulation that there can be no commercial advertising through the public schools, the administrator has the ticklish job of deciding whether the book is more educational or more a piece of advertising. If it is an especially good learning device, he might gamble on over-looking this particular advertising. If he decides he can, and puts the literature into the hands of pupils, he is certain to hear about it from a competitor in the field. More than one superintendent has had reactions from competing motor companies if their teachers happened to receive a Ford Foundation fellowship. And the local Ford agent might hint at the merits of a Ford automobile for school officials. Breathes there a superintendent who has not been forced to squirm because of the calendars used in classrooms!

Some industrial curriculum revisers are overcoming this objection by publishing literature in the name of the entire industry. This approach makes it reasonably safe for the school to accept it, unless a competing industry finds out about it. A recollection is still clear of "safely" adopting for use an exceptionally effective booklet on natural resources produced by a coalition of petroleum companies—safe until manufacturers of other fuels got wind of it. The booklet suddenly became propaganda.

Another large source of private interest curriculum revisers is found among the many charitable, moral, and somewhat educational promoters. Included among these are the numerous types of safety programs: home safety, safety on the highway, safety in the shops, safety from fire, and safety from baddies. Then there is the huge category of charitable campaigns: United Appeal, Tuberculosis, Red Cross, March of Dimes, Easter seals, to say nothing of community organizations pushing a benefit project for the handicapped. The graveling dilemma in refusing these requests is that they are all worthwhile. The superintendent is un-civic-minded, or just plain cold hearted, if he turns them down, or prejudiced if he accepts some and not all.

Reasons for Interest in the Curriculum

The first step in coping with the variety of volunteer revisers of the curriculum is to understand their motives. Why are so many different persons and groups interested in having the curriculum added to, altered, or depleted? The superintendent must analyze the cause of each request.

Educators are prone to say, "The public wants it." Who is the public? There is no such thing as *the* public; there are many publics in a community, classified in numerous ways. The publics of parents, of non-parents, of old, middle-aged, or young parents. The publics of professional personnel, of industrialists, of retailers, of labor unionists, of office workers. The publics of scholars, of athletes, of ministers, of bridge players, of Rotarians, of musicians. The publics of different colors and different religious tenets, and different political loyalties. It is no more logical to lump together all people not employed by the board of education under the label of "the public" than it is to ignore individual differences among pupil abilities. While there are threads of parallelism among these groups, each has a purpose of its own. Probably no two of them would define the objectives of education identically. With this in mind it is only natural to expect that these groups would plan differing destinies for their public schools.

To understand the pressures on the curriculum, educators must also remind themselves periodically that they are involved in a public function. All of the publics cited above, and more, own the public schools. The practice of school personnel to say "my school," "my pupils," "my textbooks," "my room," "my teachers," leads to delusive attitudes regarding the relationship of citizens to the schools. On the other hand, few citizens ever forget that the schools are public, that they are *theirs*. Therefore, they feel they have a right to make suggestions as to what their children will learn—as they certainly do.

Furthermore, Americans take a mixed, sometimes contradictory posture where their public institutions are concerned. They can be proud of them, they can respect them, they can even demonstrate awe toward public institutions and organizations; at the same time they can despise them, curse them, decry them, and suspect them. The typically ironic attitude of Americans regarding their public schools is exemplified by the realtor who opposes increased property taxes for school buildings and yet, as a sales point, capitalizes on the fact that a house is located in a district with a beautiful new building; or by the citizen who fights a bond issue but drives a stranger past the new school buildings on a Sunday afternoon to show him the highlights of the community; or by a chamber of commerce that bucks increased school taxes but lures a new industry to town by boasting of its excellent school system.

Still another reason people are interested in the curriculum is the fact that it costs money, *their* money, and a substantial amount of it if it is any good. No one likes taxes. No one likes to invest money in an enterprise from which a dividend is not forthcoming within a reasonably short time. Since they must spend money for this service called education, they want to know what those educators are doing with it.

Another common reason for wanting the curriculum changed is traced to personal occupational failures. Few graduates of any school have the gallantry to admit that they made the wrong choice of training, that they didn't work too hard in school, or, heaven forbid, that they didn't have the wherewithal to rate high scholastically. When any of these faults, or similar ones, end in vocational casualty, there must be announced a whipping boy to save face. It may be poor teaching, or poor schools, but nearly always it is some defect in the curriculum.

Akin to this reason for attacking the curriculum is that of parents whose children are not succeeding in school, either while the youngsters are in the public schools or later in college. Something has to be wrong somewhere if the child is not to blame, so it is frequently the curriculum.

The existence of national emergencies has previously been cited as an explanation of why people turn their attention to the kind of experiences children are having in school.

Superintendents must also realize that lack of understanding is a psychological reason for people to be suspicious. Individuals tend to dislike that which they do not comprehend. If citizens are not informed of what is taught and how it is being taught, they are quick to criticize if a plan misfires. School administrators, spending and having spent all their lives in an educational environment, are generally unaware of the factual famine existing among laymen regarding schools and education. The failure of school officials to keep citizens informed about their schools accounts for more criticism than any other factor.

Still another source of attack on the school curriculum is the small number, but wide variety, of people in any community who are just looking for something to criticize. They may be of little influence but they are still existent under the pseudonymns of crackpots, cranks, hardheads, or jerks. The only time they pose any serious threat to the progress of the curriculum is when things aren't going well in the school system anyhow, or when there is some doubt in the air as to the school officials' ability to run the system. It is then that the sometimes wild accusations of misanthropes may be believed by enough people to cause harm.

A final group of critics may be found among the sincere citizens who have no ax to grind but are conscientiously concerned with improving education. They may be intellectuals, ordinary citizens, or a minority group. These are the people with whom an alert superintendent can cooperate toward genuinely sound curriculum development if he doesn't erroneously associate their motives with that of all the other brands of critics.

It is essential that the superintendent patiently and astutely analyze each source of suggested revisions to the curriculum before he can deal with it.

How To Cope with the Volunteer Curriculum Revisers

For cope with them he must or else float down the circuitous stream into a whirlpool of learning activities. Although interest in, and criticism of, what goes into children's minds will never terminate, as indeed it should not, successful superintendents have been able to capitalize on the interest to accomplish educational progress and to block the recurring gimcrack notions that would sidetrack the basic functions of public education.

One of the most effective approaches to the problem is for the superintendent to "beat 'em to the draw" by opening the door to what is going on in the classroom. He is only inviting criticism if he should attempt to hide any school activity, or even if he should be innocently neglectful of keeping people informed. The publics can be kept informed by various methods, and the

superintendent should not stop with just one. The devices of
take-home leaflets and annual reports, written in simple language, which explain what and how children learn have been
found to be exceedingly beneficial for this purpose. Advice on
how to prepare these brochures is available in the chapter dealing with public relations. The effectiveness of the informing
approach was demonstrated in several school systems which
never felt the flare-up about Johnny's reading ability. Parents in
those communities knew that their children could read, and
also knew something about the modern methods of teaching
reading, because the superintendent had already told them over
and over again.

Some superintendents use PTA meetings for explaining to
parents the methods used by teachers instead of wasting the
valuable time of everyone present in determining how the unit
might spend $1.65.

Other superintendents have used citizens' committees most
effectively for keeping the public informed of educational
techniques and problems. Not only do these organizations keep
abreast of trends in this manner but the device is also of substantial psychological value in that people are "for it" if they
have a part in developing it. In organizing these curriculum
committees the superintendent should include the critics. Even
if the latter are not won over, the levelheaded members of the
committee will help to take the superintendent off the hook.

Although the superintendent ofttimes fights a hopeless battle
in dealing with the would-be athletic curriculum revisers, there
are a few effective measures suggested here. When the clamors
become persistent for more elaborate athletic provisions, he
can gather fortification for a saner approach by conducting
a community survey of parents' wishes regarding sports. It has
long been recognized that the clangorous sports fans are a decided minority. The majority of parents will speak up through
a questionnaire.

Referring matters to an athletic or curriculum advisory

board will stop many of the individual demands for radical and immediate changes in the high school sports picture.

A single boisterous agitator can frequently be silenced by inviting him to run for the board of education so that he might conduct athletics as he wishes. Most persons of this caliber will run miles in the opposite direction to avoid assuming responsibility for the program.

Another good measure for assuaging the excited critics is to invite them to school affairs. Much of the criticism is based on nothing more than superficiality. The critic of an alleged feeble music program could be sent free tickets to the next choir or band production; the man who cries publicly that spelling "ain't what it used to be" could be invited to attend an eighth grade spell down or he could be challenged to a spelling contest with high school students; the downtown quarterback who bemoans de-emphasis of football should be invited to the elementary gym show or physical education class; and the patriot who worries about liberal propaganda being disseminated in modern textbooks should be asked to serve on the textbook selection committee. In one community where the fever ran high on this point, the American History Textbook Committee sent all sample copies to the Legion Americanism Committee for evaluation and recommendation. The two committees, working separately, recommended the same book for adoption by the board of education.

Educators must develop such confidence in their training programs that they need never be fearful of exposing them to the entire populace. Not only will this attitude build confidence in what the administrator is doing, but occasionally he will receive a meritorious idea that might not otherwise have occurred to him.

Another method of building public confidence in the school's curriculum is to give releases on outstanding college scholastic achievements by former high school graduates. Any school with any curriculum can find evidences of commendable attainment among its graduates. A good school will find many. Most universities are pleased to cooperate in supplying this data for it is good public relations for them, also. An active high school guidance program will conduct frequent surveys among its graduates. In some communities where these techniques have been used over a period of years the citizens are so proud of their schools that the critics can scarcely find a sympathetic ear. There is nothing charlatanic in putting one's best foot forward; critics are not reticent to point out the worst foot.

In coping with the numerous self-interest groups that are desirous of crowding propaganda and contests into the curriculum, the need for written policies covering curriculum revision becomes obvious. Most of the requests are directed to the superintendent and only rarely to the board of education. If the superintendent and board have taken the time to formulate sound policies governing alterations to the curriculum, the superintendent can merely cite the board policy and thereby terminate the urging for a quick change. Few of the contest pushers will go over the superintendent's head if they know the board has already reflected upon the matter and has established policy. As a precautionary measure it should be pointed out that the process of establishing these policies should be accomplished during an unhurried period of time and not when the administration is being pressured by an issue of the moment.

Many of the suggestions for curriculum changes are momentary crushes that laymen develop on an idea to solve a temporary concern of theirs. Recent examples are the concerns about juvenile delinquency, shortage of engineers, neglect of mentally retarded children, and rejections from military service for physical unfitness. Frequently, the crushes develop from a solution suggested by a speaker or syndicated columnist who is totally unfamiliar with the years of research that have produced sound conclusions regarding child development, mental processes, and teaching techniques. The idea may appear logical to laymen equally unfamiliar with the research and who take up the battle-cry for change. This process makes mandatory for the superintendent a knowledge of educational history and psychological research. He can scarcely hope to combat these unscientific brainstorms unless he can support his arguments with facts. There are very few ideas for educational improvement advanced by laymen which have not been tried and tested.

Still another useful device for dealing with the periodic pressures of curriculum tamperers is a curriculum committee that meets not more often than once a month. When the reviser wants to insert something questionable into the curriculum and refuses to accept the superintendent's negative response, the latter can satisfy the immediate pressure by offering to refer the matter to the curriculum committee for study. Many unwholesome ideas can become lost in committee, and again, the decision is removed from the shoulders of one person. Just the knowledge that it will be some time before a decision is reached is enough to discourage some tamperers.

Unsolicited Revision Is Not Without Glory

With all the time-consuming torture a superintendent suffers from the voluntary curriculum revisers, there is one consolation. The extent of multifarious interest shown in education establishes the importance of the superintendency position in the eyes of the community. If one enjoys playing upstage, he'll be happy in the job.

chapter six

Quarterbacking the Administrative Team

Much similarity can be found between the methods of operation of a modern school superintendent and of football's modern T quarterback.

A reliable quarterback masterminds the action; so should a superintendent. The quarterback evaluates his team's progress after each play, appraises the opposition, checks the timing, perhaps seeks a signal from the coach, accepts suggestions from his teammates in the huddle, and then calls the play. While each step is important for his success, it should be underscored that *he calls the play*.

An effective superintendent follows these same procedures. He is constantly evaluating the progress of the administrative staff's last action; he is alert to the forces that might block his team's action; he knows that accurate timing of every new plan is as important as the idea itself; he looks to the board for counsel; he goes into a huddle with his staff specialists at regular intervals to solicit their contributions to the decision at hand; and then makes the decision. Regardless of who or what influenced the decision, it is *his* decision.

This point bears elaboration in the current rage for democratic administration. Devotees of shared decision-making may recoil from the contention that the decision must be the superintendent's, but as will be demonstrated later, there is a difference between responsibility for decision-making and the process of forming the decision. There need be no conflict between philosophies at this juncture.

THE QUARTERBACK AND SUPERINTENDENT ARE RESPONSIBLE

Look again at the quarterback. He receives the plaudits if the play is executed successfully; he also takes the blame if it fails. The tackle may have missed the block, the end may have cut too soon to be where the ball was after the quarterback threw the pass, or any one of his colleagues may have missed his assignment; nevertheless, it is clear in next day's newspaper who is held responsible for the team's dismal strategy. The coach, or even the quarterback, may remove a player whose performance holds up the team's progress more than once or twice, but still the quarterback is responsible.

It is inescapable that the superintendent, too, will be the recipient of roses or thorns depending upon the outcome of his strategy. The director of elementary education may devise a plan, carry it out with the superintendent's endorsement, and thereby achieve a substantial improvement in third grade learning, but the man in the street will give credit to that brilliant superintendent. The director of secondary education might fabricate a new system of reports to parents which blows up in his face, but the parents call the superintendent to complain. If either subordinate muffs the ball often, the superintendent, or even the board, may send in a substitute—permanently.

Responsibility for the team's action is more manifest for the superintendent than for the quarterback. Not only does the public think of the superintendent as being responsible, but if the board is fulfilling its proper evaluative role, it holds the superintendent directly responsible for all results of the staff.

Sportswriters and fans impose upon the quarterback an unwarranted morale problem by singling him out for praise. A leader worthy of the title combats this problem by extending generous and sincere recognition to his teammates, letting them know that regardless of the headlines, he knows who deserves the credit. Likewise, the successful educational leader has congratulated his lieutenant for a commendable action long before the latter reads about the "superintendent's" achievement in the newspaper. This practice of securing joint decision, giving credit where due, and issuing the decision in the superintendent's name, is the means by which the apparent conflict between executive authority and democratic administration can be reconciled.

Moreover, the modern T quarterback merely plans the strategy for others to carry the ball. In most games today he can be spotted on the field by his clean uniform. While the superintendent may not be able to boast of an unsoiled wardrobe, his release to the press gives proper recognition to the assistant who carried the ball. He invites them to board meetings for a direct report on their successful actions, and repeatedly shoves them into the public foreground. In fact, as one superintendent puts it, the top executive is doing his best job when it appears to his administrative staff that he does nothing.

THE QUARTERBACK AND SUPERINTENDENT NEED NOT BE THE BRIGHTEST TEAM MEMBER

Frequently, the quarterback is the brainiest man on the squad, but not always. He may possess other talents which qualify him for the allied duties of the position. If so, the coach may call the plays, or perhaps a lineman might size up the situation and determine the maneuver. Brilliance, isolated from concomitant abilities, may not produce a good quarterback. Witness the number of Phi Beta Kappans who sit in the bleachers.

By the same token, it would be ideal if the superintendent could parade all the essential qualities of administrative leadership as well as the highest IQ on the staff. Such is the exception, however. Nor is it mandatory that it be so. Better than average intellectual power is required, but it needn't be the highest. No set of criteria for the top executive office of any organization, whether it be formulated by rank and file, by staff, or by outsiders, ever lists high IQ in the Number One position. This fact spotlights again the inordinate importance of personal qualities that make for successful administrators. The good administrator knows how to select brainy staff members and how to create the environment in which their talents can function at the maximum. This is what makes the superintendent look brainy.

BOTH MUST FOLLOW THROUGH

One final analogy. The quarterback hasn't finished his task when he gets rid of the ball; he must execute either deception or a block. Likewise, the superintendent must follow through after making the decision. He must pave the way for a colleague to discharge the assignment, or he may personally carry out a portion of the plan. He also needs to observe and evaluate the progress.

Organizing the Staff

The administrative staff is more analogous to the football team's forward wall than to the backfield. The offensive line's sole function is to clear the way for the ball carriers. The central staff's distinctive objective is to facilitate classroom instruction. The reverse philosophy is found too often among staff personnel, and constitutes the most serious threat to staff–teacher harmony. Promotion to administrative rank is sometimes interpreted more as an honor than an opportunity to serve. A superintendent will do well to remind himself and his lieutenants frequently that the only justification for their positions is that of servicing those who carry the ball—the teachers.

Many sincere efforts have been made by school administrators over the years to diagram staff organization and operations. Volumes have been written on how to do it. One conclusive fact stands out from all these undertakings—none of them work!

The only setting in which an organization chart on paper can operate successfully in practice is old-line military, which disappeared in the 1920's. Contemporary American armies function with line control but staff decision. Probably the greatest strength of American troops in action was the resourcefulness of her buck privates when the commanders became casualties, a product of American individualistic philosophy fostered by the public schools.

Even an industry as large as the Republic Steel Corporation has abandoned the formal organization chart. The president reports:

As businesses grow in size and complexity, the urge toward regimentation is enticing. But we believe that the urge should be resisted. Rigid organizational charts, and hard and fast divisions of function and responsibility at the departmental level stunt individual growth and development.

We believe this so thoroughly at Republic that we have no formal organization chart, and we strive continually to find new ways to increase the flexibility of inter-departmental relations.

In our effort to achieve this goal, we start out with a double premise. First, that the individual must assume full responsibility for his work. This carries with it the corollary that he must receive full recognition for work well done. Second, that the prime responsibility of every man, whatever his title or rank, is to see that his job is done in terms of the best interests of the company as a whole regardless of the effect on his individual department, division or district.[1]

CONFLICT BETWEEN EFFICIENCY AND ORGANIZATION

In the building of staff organization, there exist two opposing pressures for the superintendent to reconcile. On the one

[1] T. F. Patton. "Our Greatest Asset: People." An address before the fall Personnel Conference of the American Management Association. Republic Steel Corporation, Cleveland, Ohio. Sept. 23, 1957.

hand there is the pressure for efficiency, to get the jobs done and to serve classroom teachers quickly. Nothing develops more certainly a cynical attitude among teachers toward the central staff bureaucracy than delays and buck-passing in satisfying their needs. The titles for the central staff which originate in teachers' rest rooms—"Whitehouse," "Pentagon," or "Commissioners"—are justified frequently. The larger the system, the larger the office staff becomes, and the more likely is the tendency for bureaucracy.

The classroom teachers constitute the production department of an educational organization. All other employees are instruments for helping them. Let us suppose a teacher is out of chalk. All she wants is a few pieces of chalk—and now! In the small, unorganized system she may walk fifty feet to the stock room and help herself. She is contented with this aspect of her work because her objectives are unhampered by red tape.

Now suppose the same teacher moves to a higher paying position in a systematized city school district. She also needs chalk. She sends a pupil a hundred feet and two flights of stairs to the stock room which is guarded by lock and key and the principal's secretary. The secretary sends a note back with the child, "We're fresh out. Mr. Principal and I forgot to restock. Please make out a requisition in triplicate and we'll order it from the central stock room."

Since she can't leave her classroom until after school, the requisition is not completed until late afternoon, too late for the daily delivery truck. One day gone! The original and duplicate go to the business manager for approval and recording. It happens to be a busy day for his secretary, so she doesn't get around to the transaction until the following day, at which time the original copy boards the delivery truck en route to the central stock room. Three days gone! The stock manager's order filler is home with the flu, so he postpones trifling requests until he can get at them the next day. Then, as he stamps the order "Filled" and files it, he is moved to observe, "Why can't those tomfool teachers and principals think ahead and consolidate their orders!" Four days gone!

On the fifth day a box of chalk is loaded on the delivery truck for its circuitous ride to the building, where the janitor, when time permits, carries it to the stock room, where the secretary files the pink copy and notes that the item has been received, and may or may not notify the teacher who wanted the chalk last week. The system is organized, but certainly not efficient. The teacher's attitude needs no embellishment by this time.

The same situation might obtain if a teacher needs to have a pupil tested by the psychologist, or if she has a question about her sick leave, or if she needs technical help on presenting a particular learning unit, or if she wants a leaky faucet repaired, or if she wants to consult with the art supervisor, or if she has any other wants of the one hundred or more services which the central staff is prepared to provide. Most teachers are not unreasonably demanding in their requests for materials and services, but when they request, they want it *now*. And generally they are entitled to it now.

While the superintendent's challenge here is not impossible, it is difficult. He must develop a system that provides efficient service for the teacher but avoids unbusinesslike procedures and chaos. This, then, is the other opposing pressure. He must account for expenses in a manner acceptable to the board, the auditors, and the public. No school's budget can afford a host of central personnel specialists who sit in waiting to respond promptly to teachers' beckons. Normally, each administrator has a set of tasks to complete and he operates on a schedule that can't be interrupted incessantly. The superintendent must find the happy medium.

TYPES OF ORGANIZATION

Despite teachers' occasional allusions to autocratic administrators, there is only a paucity of superintendents who operate in the strictly line fashion as shown in Figure I.

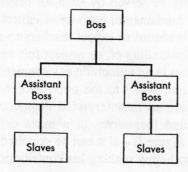

Figure I. Administrative organization chart for absolute line control

Line control is unquestionably the most efficient system. Responsibilities are clear, every person in the organization knows his duties and limitations, authority is simple, and the jobs get done. By the same token, creativeness, resourcefulness, voluntary contributions, and shared decision-making are repudiated. There are groups in society whose purpose could conceivably be served by such an organization, but it denies the most fundamental purpose of education and democratic ideals. It is absurd to expect teachers to develop among children an understanding of, or respect for, basic freedoms if they must function in an autocratic environment.

In the pendulum swing to the opposite extreme, some superintendents have so misinterpreted democratic administration that they find themselves in a maze organization that would resemble Figure II—if it can be sketched at all.

Everyone is so happy making his contribution that there is no time for work; and no one worries about it except the parents who wonder why Johnny isn't learning.

Superintendents flounder in designing their organization chart by failing to distinguish between authority and function, between channels for command and democratic operation. The former can be charted, the latter cannot. There is nothing undemocratic about channels of authority. Any organization of three or more people demands lines of command, and it has them even though they may not be predetermined or platted. In the friendly, uncharted association of as few as three people who make all decisions in joint consultation, there is inevitably the strongest personality whose opinion emerges into accepted action. As the organization involves more people, the more pronounced the channels of authority will become, until eventually the need for communication as well as for getting the task accomplished makes mandatory a formal chart of command.

For organizing command, therefore, a simple line process is adequate and necessary. Such a plan for a school system with approximately ten thousand pupils is shown in Figure III.

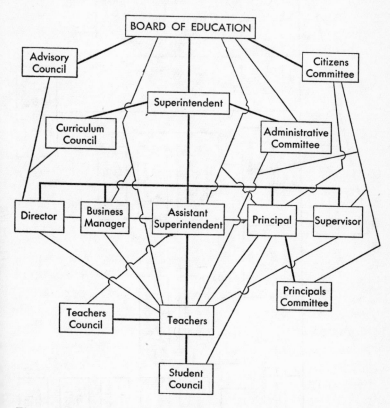

Figure II. Administrative organization chart under confused theory
of Democratic administration

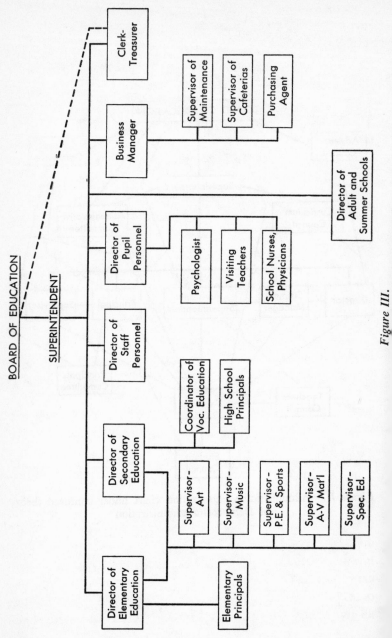

Figure III.

118

FACTORS TO CONSIDER IN ESTABLISHING
AN ORGANIZATION CHART

The organization suggested in Figure III would suffice for hundreds of school systems of comparable size, but if one were to examine the charts in existence in those systems, he would discover general similarities but no two of identical structure. The framework upon which a superintendent decides is influenced by local interests—of the board, the staff, or the public—by strengths of administrative personnel, by available finances, and by the superintendent's tastes or emphases he desires.

Some school systems may not want all the services listed in the suggested chart; others would want more. Some school districts could not afford to provide the services allowed in the chart. It does not necessarily mean that there is less need for the service, but merely that the superintendent must weigh values and decide which ones can be omitted with the least harm to the educational program.

Titles of administrative officers vary among school systems, even though functions may be similar. A director in X City may be a supervisor in Y City or a coordinator or consultant in Z City. Some superintendents would prefer one or two assistant superintendents responsible directly to them with all other executives responsible to the assistant.

THE ASSISTANT SUPERINTENDENT

Having one assistant superintendent in a hypothetical system the size of which is presently being considered presents unnecessary headaches to the superintendent which a slightly different organization could avoid. If the assistant stands in the line of command between the superintendent and all junior executives, it raises the question in the minds of teachers and of economy-minded citizens, "What's the superintendent doing all this time?" On the other hand, if there is an assistant superintendent in charge of one phase of the administrative program, be it personnel, business, curriculum, or whatnot, while other functions are being handled by lesser rank, it means that the superintendent has assigned a value to one function higher than others—this is difficult to swallow by the administrators of other departments.

Some superintendents have attempted to evade these criticisms by appointing an assistant *to* the superintendent. As much as the need may be evident for such position, few taxpayers are willing to admit it.

Another factor entering into the decision of whether there is to be an assistant superintendent is the chief executive's predilection for desk work or field work. Some superintendents prefer the paper phase of administration, sometimes labeled "executive" work, and need an assistant to handle people. Others of a more gregarious nature can't stand lifting paperweights or the confinements of an upholstered swivel chair. Since both functions are necessary and since the proper blend of the two is rarely found in one man, the superintendent must either appoint an assistant or else reshuffle duties among his administrative team.

HOW MANY ASSISTANTS SHOULD BE RESPONSIBLE DIRECTLY TO THE SUPERINTENDENT?

In considering the pattern of organization the superintendent must find a balance between the burden resulting from an excessive number of assistants reporting directly to him and the handicap of not keeping informed because of an insufficient number of subordinates to report on the diversified functions involved in the administration of a sizable school system. Industrial management, having been concerned with this problem for many years, has pioneered with research. Their conclusion is that an executive in a medium to large organization cannot handle efficiently more than eight assistants. Beyond this point there must be reorganization of function and title.

ORGANIZATION INFLUENCED BY INDIVIDUAL ABILITIES

Probably the most significant factor in determining staff organization is the respective strengths and weaknesses of staff persons on the payroll. No astute administrator can overlook this aspect, and an even less astute superintendent will be unconsciously influenced by it. The more capable staff member will be assigned either the most difficult or the most important function, and there is no stopping his rise to the challenge. Differences that exist in administrative organization among school systems of similar size are accounted for more by individual differences in the power of staff members than by any other factor.

THE ORGANIZATION MUST ALLOW FLEXIBILITY

It is behooving to point out for the benefit of a certain type of superintendent the danger of worshiping organization at the sacrifice of efficiency and good judgment. The organization chart is merely a device for getting the job done, not an end in itself. For some administrators, once an idea is assigned to black and white, it becomes holy. Actually, the need for flexibility and occasional violations of channels of command are desirable in any organization, but especially so in one devoted to teaching democratic concepts.

While a flexible organization is undoubtedly the most productive, its successful operation is predicated upon the ability of staff members to work harmoniously. The gadfly who will upset such an organization is the cantankerous, selfish, ill-humored, or insecure associate. Some people can't function in a give-and-take environment. They may be successful in solo operations, but can't work as a team except through black and white directives. Such a person can cause a cancerous condition that will generate enough internal friction to nullify the effects of the organization. The only cure, if one is to preserve the strength of an organization operating with individual freedom and initiative, is to remove the cancer.

THE PLACE OF THE BUSINESS FUNCTION
IN THE CHANNEL OF COMMAND

Usually there is no more unsatisfactory assignment in school administration than the business and financial responsibilities. Even when the position is filled with a person acceptable to the superintendent, it is a constant source of friction with the staff and faculty. They refuse to accept it as an important element of education.

In recent years the business and financial aspects of school administration have assumed a status of gigantic proportions, and one which demands an undue share of the superintendent's day. With spiraling enrollments and costs, diminishing sources of revenue per pupil, increasing public resistance to more taxes, rapid construction of school buildings, and substantial purchasing of supplies and equipment, the superintendent has been compelled to become a fiscal expert more than an educator. Public school operations have become one of the largest businesses that exist in most communities.

Since this book does not intend to deal with the legal and technical aspects of school business and finance, only the organization and personnel factors will be discussed.

SHOULD THE BUSINESS MANAGER BE
AN EDUCATOR OR A BUSINESSMAN?

A major decision in selecting a business manager is the choice between an expert in business management without educational orientation or a schoolman without business training. The precise seasoning of both backgrounds is seldom uncovered under one skin.

Although purchasing agents or maintenance men who have been grounded in industrial experience bring contacts and some desirable techniques to the school situation, few can adjust to the school business function. Their sense of economy and ethics is geared more to profit making and cost accounting objectives. This is not to censure either profit making or economy. Most school administrators have been forced to learn more about stretching a dollar than their industrial counterparts. Frequently, however, the school purchasing agent with an industrial background cannot understand why an economical purchase for a production plant would not always be an economy for a learning situation. One such business manager of the author's acquaintance insists today that textbooks should be purchased on competitive bid, the contract going to the low bidder.

There are numerous facets of a school situation which the industrial-minded business manager finds difficult to comprehend: the urgency for having materials on hand when they are needed to assure a smooth continuation of the learning process being as important as the need for having factory supplies on hand in time to prevent production interruptions; the sensitivity and intellectual stature of school personnel which relieves the business manager of the necessity to curse or shout to win their cooperation; the need for a public school to maintain community good will by dealing with local merchants and by distributing purchases with reasonable equity when comparable price and quality conditions can be assured; the scorn with which educators look upon kickbacks and favors from vendors; or the necessity to operate within a strict annual budget knowing that there is no possibility for additional revenue as there might be in industry.

The author's observation is that the business skills are easier to learn than the educational philosophy. Therefore, generally it is better to promote a schoolman who gives evidence of good business judgment and the ability to learn purchasing, budgeting, and maintenance techniques.

ASSIGNMENT OF THE CLERK-TREASURER OR FISCAL SECRETARY OF THE BOARD

To a lesser degree the same problems are present in the selection of a clerk-treasurer, or secretary, to the board of education. No other organization in our society, private or public, handles its fiscal affairs exactly as a board of education must do. Practically every expenditure is governed by state law, which is not always compatible with common sense, efficiency, or expediency. Many months, sometimes years, are required for a stranger to school legal and financial procedures to become comfortable in managing the board's affairs. It is unfortunate that few boards hold this position in high enough esteem to allow a salary that will attract the caliber of person required to do the job intelligently.

A once common problem of assigning the posts of business manager and clerk-treasurer in the central staff framework of command causes few concerns any more. Most boards and superintendents have made the officers responsible to the superintendent, as they unquestionably should be. Instances are rare, perhaps unknown, in which any organization can function efficiently under dual command, especially if he who controls the purse strings is independent of the commander-in-chief. There is some justification for having the clerk-treasurer at least partially responsible directly to the board of education; some state laws require it. This arrangement works well as long as it is understood that the clerk's function is to account for funds, not to determine how they shall be spent.

DEVELOPING COMPATIBILITY BETWEEN PROFESSIONAL AND BUSINESS FUNCTIONS

As important as the business and fiscal phases of school operations have become, superintendents must wage a continual struggle to maintain these functions in their proper perspective of the total educational organization. Handling sizable sums of money ofttimes gives the business manager or fiscal agent an unwarranted sense of power.

These officers have a psychological handicap in carrying out the superintendent's directives by virtue of the fact that they are usually the ones who have to say "No" to numerous requests. This is never a popular assignment, but it can be made more painless by saying it in a professional tone. Many business managers and school fiscal agents must be reminded again and again that they, too, are merely tools for the education of boys and girls.

That staff members do not bear ardent affection for the business officers is not entirely the fault of the latter. Generally, no one but the superintendent has an understanding and appreciation of the work and problems of these officers. The most common cause of all friction—misunderstanding—obtains also in the relationships between the professional staff and the business departments. Obviously, the only means for overcoming this friction is by promoting understanding.

This is not easy in the busy schedules of all persons involved, but it can be helped by better communication, by giving reasons when saying, "No," and by exchanging assignments if possible. Understudies to the fiscal agents are arranged for in some school systems. One of the requirements in a good administrative intern program is for the budding executive to spend time with the business manager and clerk-treasurer. Teacher training institutions could be of inestimable value in solving this problem by requiring at least one course for all teachers in school law and finance.

Defining Function

After the type of organization has been determined and the flow of control has been charted, there still remains an important step in achieving efficient operations of the central staff for servicing teachers. Duties of each officer must be spelled out in as much detail as possible. The larger the staff, the more vital this step becomes.

It is equally important for each person to know what he is not supposed to do as well as what he is to do. One of the two primary purposes of having the duties of each officer written out is to avoid stepping on the other fellow's toes. Even when desirable human relations obtain among members of the staff, no one likes to have a colleague entering his sphere of operations. When responsibilities are defined clearly, it is a relatively simple matter to settle disputes of jurisdiction.

The other primary reason for the listing is to facilitate teachers' knowing where to go for their various wants. This, again, is more essential in large systems where the officials perform in more specialized roles. A teacher should be able to refer to her booklet of administrative duties to learn quickly whom she should call for library books, for art paper, for the speech and hearing therapist services, for hospitalization information, and for the myriad of other needs that develop during the year.

It is impossible, of course, to be so comprehensive in the definition of duties as to include all aspects of the job that will arise. Moreover, the nature of the position will probably alter with the passing of time. It is common practice to list as the final duty, "All other pertinent responsibilities as assigned by the superintendent."

Every member of the administrative staff, the faculty, and the board should have a copy of the duties, and they should be available to the public when requested.

While each superintendent will want to develop his own set of duties appropriate to his system, he may obtain help as to style, scope, and nature by writing to nearly any city school system for sample copies or by consulting the nearest university's department of educational administration.

Written Policies

Still a third necessity for efficient operations in a larger school system is the written statement of board regulations and administrative policies that affect all segments of the teaching corps. In fact, this production could well be the most essential step.

Written policies are needed for answering the frequent problems that arise from day to day, for speedy orientation of new faculty and staff members, for achieving uniformity of procedures, for providing continuity in practice, and for settling disputes that will develop.

With all the recent urging of school superintendents to adopt written statements of policies and despite the mass of literature explaining how to do it properly, there is still a surprising dearth of accomplished projects. A likely reason for this neglect is that much of the writing and lecturing makes the job appear too formidable. Actually, there is little difficulty involved; time-consuming perhaps, but not prostrating.

In undertaking the task the superintendent needs to have clearly in his own mind what a policy is. A practical definition of a policy for this purpose is merely "a way of dealing with a matter that is likely to arise frequently." An administrative ruling that Teacher X cannot attend this year's NEA Convention, or a board decision that textbook A is unsuitable for adoption in American History, are not policies. These are strictly rulings covering isolated situations that are unlikely to recur. However, decisions that no teacher will be permitted to attend the NEA conventions or that fused social studies textbooks will not be tolerated in American history classes, do constitute policies.

The task of developing a set of written policies becomes quite simple when the document is interpreted as nothing more than an organized list of guides which govern the common actions of teachers and administrators. Most school systems already have the majority of policies in effect, either from formal action taken by the board, administrative fiat, or through practice. Assembling these policies into an organized, indexed publication is just a matter of taking the time to pull them together into some logical and readable form. The style, grammar, scope, type of printing, and cover are not of monumental significance.

If the job has never been done for a school system, the superintendent, or person delegated to do the job, in assembling the data will undoubtedly find conflicting policies in effect, some out of date, and some acceptable procedures that have never been stated as a policy. Common sense dictates how these matters are solved.

The literature has much to say about how the policies must be made jointly with innumerable committees studying this and that phase of the project. In the original determination of a policy, the superintendent may engage as many coadjutors as he sees fit, as long as he doesn't democratize to the point of never completing the job; but this has nothing to do with assembling the policies into publishable form. In fact, committees retard the process of composing and assembling. It is recommended that only one person be assigned the task of arranging the material into a semi-completed form and then allow a committee to analyze it and suggest corrections.

Another shortcoming in some written policy documents is the attempt to produce a handsome booklet. Judging from an examination of these publications, it would seem that superintendents ofttimes vie with each other to present their audiences with the prettiest production, if not the longest. A mimeographed production that is easy to handle is much better than an ecstatically printed and bound booklet. To be sure, the permanently bound set of written policies is the least desirable. It is inexcusable to find beautiful policy handbooks full of fusty policies cluttering the desk drawers of school personnel. While one of the purposes of written policies is to achieve uniformity and consistency, the principal characteristic of any policy should be its changeability. The danger of putting policies into writing is the tendency to consider them fixed forever. Practices must change to keep pace with progress, and the simple loose leaf-notebook, therefore, provides the best arrangement for keeping policies flexible and up to date.

A final emphasis in the preparation of written policies is the urgency for simplicity, some sensible arrangement of items, and indexing if the publication consists of more than just a few pages. A helpful device is a section that could be entitled "Whom To Contact For What."

Delegation of Authority

The greatest uphill struggle a superintendent experiences with himself in the building of an efficient administrative team, particularly for the man who came up the customary ladder from a smaller school system, is to develop a willingness to release the reins to his subordinates. This is a problem common to all conscientious persons. It is observed among teachers who refuse to stay home when they are ill for fear a substitute will foul up their lesson plans. Some teachers fail in their efforts to develop the leadership capacity among students through permitting them to assume responsibilities because they fear the tasks will not be done as well as they would do them. It is the same fear that prevents many superintendents from creating an efficient organization.

The reasons for the importance of delegating duties and authority are numerous. In the first place, it is absolutely impossible for any man, however talented and energetic, to perform all the administrative operations of a large school system. It is inevitable that an undermanned administrative staff will neglect some of the educational functions which the taxpayers have a right to expect. Even medium-sized school systems which have been operating under a one-man administrative staff can be spotted immediately by the absence of a comprehensive program of educational services and accomplishments.

A selfish reason for delegating duties is to protect one's own health. The 1952 A.A.S.A. Yearbook suggests that "It is entirely probable that one of the reasons so many of the superintendents in our largest cities have retired or died prematurely in service is because they personally attempted to carry far more than one man's burden."[2]

Third, it is uneconomical to have assistants on the payroll and not let them earn their money. Also, they will never

[2] A.A.S.A. Yearbook, 1952, p. 67.

mature into effective administrators until given an opportunity to grow with responsibility, any more than pupils can mature into responsible citizens without practice. A superintendent owes his teammates the opportunity to make mistakes in order to develop. Furthermore, no administrator worth his salt enjoys working in an environment that does not permit him freedom to make decisions and carry them out. One of the distinguishing marks of the new brand of superintendent is that he is willing to make his own decisions and gamble his future on their turning out right. The failure to appreciate this same desire on the part of subordinates is a weakness that separates executives from office boys in school administration. And finally, no superintendent can afford to feel so insecure that he cannot trust others to do things correctly.

LEARNING THE ART OF DELEGATING AUTHORITY

How to overcome the reluctance to delegate authority is perplexing for an administrator devoid of self-confidence, for an egotistical one, a selfish one, or one accustomed to doing everything himself. It can't be overcome until he is willing to modify his philosophy of administration. Failure to delegate authority is really a problem of fear and distrust. A few suggestions are offered as aids in this direction.

The superintendent can try getting away from the job more often, permitting junior officers to assume command. He will be amazed, and somewhat deflated, to discover how well things run without him. A thorough job of writing out duties will assure that all aspects of his total responsibility are covered. Conferences with other administrators who have developed the proper philosophy will help. Accepting the fact that no man is indispensable is fundamental to the point of view. A man with wartime combat experience has little difficulty in acquiring the proper perspective as to his indispensability. Keeping subordinates informed of all plans and activities will enable them to carry on in the absence of the superintendent. Superintendents can also learn something from a lazy man who never worries about letting "George do it."

No large organization can function without delegating authority and duties. The modern superintendent picks his men well, defines their duties clearly, and then *lets them do the work*. He supports them in their decisions, takes public blame for their errors, but within the official family lets them know whose fault it is as certainly as a first sergeant might do.

In summary of this section, the most effective school administrative organization is one in which the superintendent is busy getting out of the way so that his assistants can do his work.

Inter-staff Communication

One of the major problems in a sizable administrative staff is assuring that the left hand knows what the right hand is doing. Technical pedagese might refer to it as horizontal communication, in contrast to vertical communication from superintendent to principal, or principal to teacher. Even with a harmonious staff, written policies, and well-defined duties it is entirely possible that two staff members may duplicate each other's actions, or even issue countermanding directions to the same teacher.

In one well-organized staff this incident happened. In talking with some of the teachers, the supervisor of elementary education had discovered a need for enriching a unit on colonial America with some audio-visual materials. In scanning the catalogues he discovered what seemed to be an appropriate set of film strips dealing with early folksongs and dances. He ordered them. What he did not know was that the supervisor of audio-visual materials had already placed an order for six sets of the same film strips, and that the director of music had anticipated the blending of Thanksgiving music with the same learning unit and had also ordered the strips. Fortunately, the system of business control caught the error before any purchasing was consummated, but the lack of horizontal communication caused unnecessary duplication of study and ordering.

In that same well-organized school system the supervisor of secondary education authorized a high school teacher to represent the school system at a distant reading conference, at a time when both funds and availability of substitutes were at a low ebb. He did not know that the supervisor of elementary education had already authorized attendance at the same conference for two elementary teachers.

Several devices are available to the superintendent for achieving satisfactory inter-staff communication without undue loss of time or motion.

"Send a note," is a good motto for the executive staff. If one has a problem, question, or action involving another, let him know about it by a brief note, assuming that the situation does not warrant a telephone call or conference. It should be emphasized that a note is called for, not a letter in quadruplicate. One director of the author's acquaintance has a complete file of all communications he has ever sent or received, properly initialed, alphabetized, stamped, and endorsed. He never gets crossed up in his orders and actions, but there is very little of the latter. He is known among his colleagues as "The Spinning File."

One superintendent demands a weekly report on work completed and work contemplated for the next week, similar to the outmoded weekly lesson plan for teachers. He also requires all purchase orders to cross his desk for approval. Thus he avoids duplication of purchases and effort on the part of his staff. However, an unreasonable amount of staff time, as well as his own, is absorbed in report writing and report reading. Furthermore, this paper control of his staff keeps *him* informed but not his assistants.

STAFF MEETINGS NECESSARY
FOR COMMUNICATION

Some form of staff meeting is essential in any large organization, but the *form* is the difference between efficient and inefficient operations. Any meeting of high priced executives to cope with matters that could be as readily handled by a bulletin is an indefensible waste of tax money. A meeting of all staff members to discuss a matter affecting only two or three persons is equally inexcusable.

Holding a meeting just because it is scheduled at regular intervals when there happen to be no matters of significance on hand is senseless and a sure method of losing staff confidence in the leadership ability of the superintendent.

Top commanders need to learn that there are various kinds of staff conferences and varying purposes for calling them. The punishment should fit the purpose.

There are unscheduled short meetings to deal with emergencies which necessitate joint opinion and decision. There are unscheduled long meetings to explore fully an idea or plan. There are scheduled regular conference meetings over an extended period of time to deal with just one problem that cannot be consummated in one long session. There are explanatory meetings at which the chairman holds forth throughout to assure that all those present thoroughly understand that which is to be explained. There are meetings just the reverse in which the participants dominate with the leader furnishing answers to questions. There are regularly scheduled staff meetings to discuss new business and old business occurring during the year. Then there is the type used entirely too seldom, the idea or brainstorming meeting, during which participants are urged to turn their imaginations loose to arrive at possible solutions to a given problem.

One type of meeting which some superintendents have found useful for the problem at hand—maintaining inter-staff communication—is a weekly short staff meeting just to report in the hearing of all executives what each is planning to ac-

complish that week. Each official in turn reports his major
objectives or problems contemplated. Occasionally a particular problem may be dealt with at some length, but the session
rarely lasts more than half an hour, sometimes not more than
fifteen minutes. Each officer knows that his problem must
concern more than one other person present or it should be
discussed at another time.

SOME ADDITIONAL GUIDES FOR SUCCESSFUL STAFF MEETINGS

Meetings should not be called, except in emergencies, without the staff knowing in advance the general nature of the
agenda.

Every meeting should have a predetermined terminal hour
known by all those summoned, so that each can plan his work
accordingly; and the appointed adjournment hour should be
respected.

The time for regularly recurring meetings should be determined jointly to suit the majority of those involved, not
just the superintendent.

The superintendent, or chairman, must curtail the partici-
pant who presses for an undue share of the group's time.

If the meeting is likely to last more than an hour, allow a
recess or coffee break.

A relaxed environment, if not carried to excess, will produce
better thinking and wider participation when desired.

Permit no interruptions short of emergencies.

Someone must be designated to inform the absent member
of action and decisions made.

Managing Executives

The ability to handle a corps of executives is another vital
skill for the successful school superintendent to master. Efforts
to manage an executive staff appear in various forms, including
the two extreme approaches. At one pole there is the kindly,
sensitive milquetoast who is so miserable with unpleasant

situations that he hides behind the nearest door marked SUPER-
INTENDENT. He does not want to offend anyone, especially
his subordinates who are doing the administrative work. It is
understandable why the profession is loaded with men of this
disposition. The warmly sympathetic nature so essential for the
process of teaching boys and girls, however, can be a detriment to the rugged role of the superintendency.

At the opposite extreme is the autocratic captain who
snoops, inspects, condemns, and punishes. Remnants of both
breeds are still at large in superintendent offices throughout the
land, some of whom will complete successful careers if the
criterion for success is never having been fired.

Other superintendents have succumbed to the psychological
technique of patting subordinates on the back in order to increase their efforts without ever riding herd. This is not to
negate the positive approach, which should be used generously.
To employ the approach exclusively, however, implies a staff
so inhumanly perfect that no one ever needs prodding by
censure. Such a staff has never come to the attention of the
author. A prospective superintendent without the courage to
"give 'em hell" occasionally had better remain in his teaching
role.

There is not even a hint intended that a superintendent has
to be mean, revengeful, or unreasonable. There is a real art
in censuring without degrading and without the censured losing respect for his superior officer; but it can be done. A
simple straight-shooting interview, laying cards face up, evad-
ing no criticisms, will usually do the trick. The superintendent
will discover that the anticipation of an unpleasant interview
is worse than the interview. He will also learn that most subordinates appreciate, even if they don't like it, having errors
and weaknesses pointed out to them. In fact, like pupils, they
expect it. There certainly is no justification for the dismissal or
demotion of any employee without warning, without having
his faults indicated previously, and without being granted a
chance to mend his ways.

The superintendent needs a bag of stimulating techniques for moving his staff, also, and a sufficient understanding of human nature to know when to utilize which technique. He has to be as conscious of individual differences among staff employees as the teacher does among her pupils. He may not always employ the correct technique for every situation, but of one fact he can be sure—no one approach to motivating effort will work for all persons or all situations.

The Quarterback Still Calls the Play

With an efficient organization, harmoniously staffed with capable personnel who understand their duties while operating independently under clear written policies and aware of the actions of colleagues, it is advisable to reiterate that the superintendent is still the quarterback. His responsibility for staff action cannot be denied. Whatever quality of service and achievement results—good, mediocre, or weak—the responsibility is the superintendent's.

There remains one further question to answer for the administrative quarterback. In this era of democratic administration, does he have the legal or moral right to overrule the decision of a subordinate executive or committee? Unequivocably, he has both.

There are still those educators at all levels who would relegate the superintendent to an executive role in the old sense, meaning "You carry out what we decide." Frequently, these are the same people who are willing for the superintendent to assume responsibility if the decision misfires.

Responsibility carries final authority. Of course, an astute superintendent will exercise judiciousness in overruling subordinate decisions, and he himself may be overruled by the board. But as long as the law and the board of education hold the superintendent responsible for all school activity, the quarterback calls the play!

chapter seven

Give the Apple Back

Giving apples to the teacher is still a popular gesture among the younger set in order to induce her good will, but the process is reversed for the modern superintendent. He, too, is vitally concerned with winning good will and, consequently, is in the year-round business of distributing shiny apples. If one were to list all the functions of a public school superintendent in order of importance, a strong case could be made for placing public relations at the top.

It may seem odd to assign such a respectable place to the public relations function in the life of one whose supposedly important contribution to society is the education of children. The assignment can be justified, however, in terms of the high correlation between good public relations and good education. Via syllogistic logic, the quality of the education of children in public schools depends directly upon good will. Good will produces the money necessary to employ the best teachers, to maintain small classes, and to provide adequate facilities, equipment, and supplies.

The quality of education is in direct ratio to the financial means of providing it. There are no short cuts. It is true that human abilities can make a mediocre school system better or a well-supported system worse. But the talent normally available in a poor school district will never make it a good system, nor will the customary weaknesses found in any school's personnel make a very bad educational program out of a wealthy school district. The basic laws of economics apply to the quality of education just the same as they do to the quality of any other service or commodity. To complete the syllogism, therefore, a school administrator's chief function is to develop community good will toward the public schools.

Educators have been tardy in recognizing the importance of wholesome public relations. In fact, it was only as we approached the middle of the twentieth century that school people doffed their cloistered robes and deliberately mixed with the man in the street. Once they started, the progress was as rapid as the acceptance of a popular song. It is only hoped the function will not fade as rapidly. Its popularity is evidenced by the number of books, articles, college courses, workshops, public relations associations, and public relations employees available throughout the country.

The successful superintendent spends approximately 50 per cent of his time in this endeavor. This may appear to be an exaggerated claim; and it is under the traditional approaches to public relations. However, the truth of the statement unfolds as a new concept of public relations is defined in the following pages.

It is not the purpose of this chapter to discuss in detail the mechanical techniques of school publicity. That has already been done adequately in numerous publications. In this chapter a different notion of public relations will be analyzed with the expectation that it will affect the direction of the superintendent's energy in his responsibility for developing community good will. Also, some basic principles of public relations will be proposed with the hope that they will enable superintendents to avoid common mistakes in achieving desirable community attitudes toward public education.

A New Concept of Public Relations

When public relations is stripped of its jargon and mysticism, it has a very simple meaning. Having good school public relations is nothing more than achieving a favorable attitude among people toward the schools. It is an attitude of people toward people. How does anyone develop favorable attitudes toward himself? Merely by making friends. In other words, good public relations is nothing more than maintaining good human relations, a worthwhile activity practiced long before the term "public relations" was conceived. Unfortunately, every person is not adept in the art of human relations, but if this concept can be accepted, let us see what any superintendent can do to build better public attitudes toward schools.

PUPILS AS A PUBLIC RELATIONS MEDIUM

The most important medium for developing wholesome attitudes toward the educational program is the student body itself. It also constitutes the largest and handiest medium. It is the most important because the one major criterion by which parents evaluate the school is the degree to which they are satisfied with the training of their children. It makes little difference what a fine personality the superintendent might be, what an exemplary philosophy guides his actions, what palatial or economical school buildings he might construct, how efficiently the system is operated, or how perfect everything about the schools may be. A parent is basically concerned with only one outcome—how does it all affect his child? Furthermore, a parent is interested not a whit in what the majority might do, nor how good other people say the school system is; the strong egoistic drive in mankind generally overrules all other instincts when the chips are down.

Recognizing this fundamental law of psychology puts a different twist on how the superintendent should allocate the time he spends on public relations. He might well worry less about what educational scandal the newspaper is propagating and concentrate more upon building a good learning program. The critical writings and speeches of education's "attackers" can make only an infinitesimal impression on the thinking of a parent whose child is happy in school and makes expected progress in learning.

TEACHERS AS A PUBLIC RELATIONS MEDIUM

The second most important medium for building favorable attitudes toward the schools is the teaching staff. A satisfied, capable corps of teachers is the fulcrum for developing contented pupils and parents. A "chicken-and-egg" argument could ensue here, but the reason for listing pupils ahead of teachers as effective public relations media is a numerical one. There are many more pupils than there are teachers in any community. The significance of numbers is also the reason that teachers are much better public relations agents than the superintendent. If the superintendent would think of each teacher as a satellite moving in its orbit of friends and acquaintances within the community, the impact of this body of personnel could be appreciated. A teacher who enjoys her work will do little complaining among her friends other than the customary American pastime of good-natured griping.

The same principle applies to noncertificated personnel as well as to teachers and subordinate administrators. The comments of secretaries, janitors, bus drivers, and cooks about the schools carry weight among each person's individual orbit of community acquaintances.

THE SUPERINTENDENT AS A PUBLIC RELATIONS MEDIUM

The third strongest influence for building public good will is the superintendent. Here, again, it could be debated who comes first. A strong educational leader, looking to the needs of his teaching staff, who produce contented pupils in turn, might be said to be fundamental to the entire process of building good will. Still, the scope of his influence is rarely that wide. Some pupils and teachers are happy and successful in spite of the superintendent, and vice versa. It becomes obvious under this concept of public relations, nevertheless, that the superintendent's first responsibility in the public relations function is with the staff and educational program.

The superintendent's next concern with public relations should be his own human relations. The previous reference to the criterion by which parents evaluate a school system also applies to their evaluation of the superintendent's effectiveness. All the good work he might accomplish, the astute speeches he might make, the efficient and economical purchasing he might achieve, or the capable teachers he might employ will benefit little a citizen's attitude toward the superintendent if the guy isn't liked. Conversely, a citizen will overlook many a short-coming in the school system, or in the superintendent's family, if he likes and respects the chief executive. The claim that this is a poor yardstick for evaluating either the school system or the superintendent cannot be disputed, but logical argument seldom defeats emotion.

Now the unfortunate aspect of this truism is that no super-intendent, nor any other man, can win 100 per cent love and respect of a community's citizenry or of the school's teaching staff. Any time a public figure makes a decision, as diplo-matic as he may be, he will have someone less happy about his existence. Some decisions result in irreconcilable enmities. It is not a hopeless situation, however. It means that the super-intendent can enjoy general good human relations in a com-munity if his decisions leave favorable tastes in the mouths of the majority, and if he moves in a variety of the community's circles so that more people can have an opportunity to discover firsthand what a decent chap he is. Every favorable contact he makes acts as the fabled ripple in the pond to spread the good word among each ripple's acquaintances.

For a superintendent to become known personally in a community entails considerable time and money. It means he must arrange his schedule so that he can get away from the office during the day for meetings, luncheons, and speaking engagements. It does not mean that he should join the boys at the lodge for a few hands in the afternoon, or chat on the street corner in the morning. Taxpayers, as well as colleagues, have decided opinions about a public servant who spreads his glad tidings downtown during office hours excessively. Building good will toward himself or the schools must be much less obvious.

It does mean many evening engagements—professional, civic, and social. A superintendent has ofttimes been defined as a person who dedicates his life to other people's children while he neglects his own. Any person who is unwilling to accept the sacrifice of time with his family should not consider public school superintendency as a livelihood. He knows no limitation of working hours. It's part of the job, part of the public relations function.

Belonging to a number of community organizations freezes a tidy share of the superintendent's pay check. The hidden expenses of club membership and his expected contributions to every charitable solicitation result in a take-home pay far less impressive than the figure as printed in the local gazette. There are three consolations: it's a step toward professional success, he has to do it anyhow, and the costs are deductible from his income tax report.

Some superintendents overdo the socializing aspect of their function to the neglect of their other duties. As in all other realms of human action, there are extremes to be avoided. A recommended pattern of joining would include church, service club, PTA, fraternal club, a social club with wife attached, plus service on a charitable or welfare board.

It is obviously impossible in a very large city for the superintendent to become personally acquainted with many of the voting public. He may still have contacts with representative groups, but must rely upon his decisions, staff, writings, and public appearances to speak for him. Television has been a boon to the superintendent for reaching the rank and file of a large city.

ORGANIZATION FOR PUBLIC RELATIONS
UNDER THE HUMAN RELATIONS CONCEPT

Currently there is extensive debate among educators over the relative merits of centralized vs. decentralized public relations organization and over the use of a public relations specialist. By centralized public relations is generally meant a planned program of releases and information emanating from a central authority of one or a few individuals. Under the concept of developing favorable human relations as defined herein the argument is settled. There can be no central control of the public relations function. There is no need for a trained publicity man, with the possible exception of very large city school systems. Practically everyone in the school system becomes a public relations practitioner, if not an expert.

Under the philosophy of decentralized public relations activities it is admittedly unrealistic to expect every member of the faculty to be a desirable source of publicity. Some teachers, though capable in the classroom, never think of their teaching as having good will potentialities. They become good will ambassadors through their work, however. There will also undoubtedly be some whose judgment or taste in deciding what constitutes appetizing public information would be questioned. Nonetheless, if a superintendent must choose between the occasional public relations blunder of a few teachers and the censorship of all, there need be little indecision under the concept proposed here and consistent with the prevailing viewpoint of democratic administration. Although it can never be proved one way or another, it is doubtful if much long-lasting harm can result from an unfortunate release by a misguided teacher.

The centralized control of school information is certainly unpopular, if acceptable at all, to established media of communication. The only reporters who like it are those who want a quick source for all school releases. Otherwise, the practice smacks too much of waving the red flag of interference in the face of the fourth estate's freedom. Moreover, it is difficult to comprehend the authority with which a superintendent attempts to prevent reporters from interviewing members of the faculty and staff.

Generally, a superintendent can achieve virtual centralized control of releases merely by letting news hawks know that they are welcome to obtain information from any source within the school system. With all appearances of censorship removed, the reporter loses his urge to get around it. He will then probably turn to the superintendent for his news, or at least clear with him, before reporting any school news.

A defense can be made for employing a public relations officer in a public school system in only a few circumstances. It can probably be justified if the superintendent's human relations capacity is at such low ebb that he does the system more harm than good by mixing publicly. It is also justified if the system is of such size that someone, who might as well be a public relations specialist, must be delegated the responsibility for developing brochures for keeping the public informed on school matters.

As a rule people are as suspicious of a public relations employee in a public school as they are of a low grade advertisement. They can even understand the latter; businesses are expected to sell their product. But why should anyone sell public education, especially pay someone out of tax money to do it? Schools certainly aren't after more customers. Then, to some minds, it occurs that the administration wants to cover up something with sweet propaganda. A sound program of public relations should be much more subtle than hiring an expert.

Another inherent danger in the "expert" approach to public relations is the same that obtains in the appointment of a specialist for any other department of the school. As soon as one person is delegated the responsibility for a service there appears a tendency for other teachers to assume that he will do all that is necessary in performing the service. A reading specialist cannot teach all the reading, a circuit music teacher cannot give all the music instruction that ought to be provided, nor can a public relations specialist build all the favorable attitudes toward schools. But the rest of the faculty thinks he can, or that he should.

Under the proposed concept of public relations for schools, therefore, there need be no organization and no personnel specifically assigned the job. It is true that the expert trained for that purpose might produce a better informational gimmick, but many members of the staff can be trained to do an acceptable job. As will be shown later, it is probably more effective in a community if the public relations materials used by a school are not too professional in appearance.

Principles for Preparation and Use of Standard Public Relations Devices

After a school system has earned a high rating in the eyes of citizens through the approach just outlined, it cannot relax. It has a continuing responsibility for keeping people informed of what is going on. Therefore, the remainder of this chapter is devoted to suggestions for improving the informational services of the school. Moreover, it is by no means assumed that all schools have arrived, or will soon arrive, at the enviable position of having all patrons enthusiastically supporting public education. There is a sizable corps of voters in any community who, through misinformation, disinterest, or antagonism, need to be kept abreast of progress and problems. The following principles can also be of help to the superintendent toward the accomplishment of this objective.

THE SUPERINTENDENT SHOULD ESTABLISH RAPPORT WITH COMMUNITY NEWS MEDIA EARLY

One of the first calls a public relations conscious superintendent makes upon his arrival in a new community will be

upon the news editors of established communication media—
newspapers, radio, and TV. During these get-acquainted visits
he should assure the editor of his willingness to supply school
news as requested, and should invite the reporters to contact
any school personnel for information. He should learn the
deadlines of the various media and let it be known that he expects to treat all of them alike. He might also get acquainted
with the reporter who normally covers school affairs.

DISTINGUISH BETWEEN GENERAL RELEASES AND DEVELOPED LEADS

A superintendent should recognize the difference that exists
in the minds of reporters between general releases and stories
rooted out by individual writers. Normally, releases from the
superintendent should be given to all communication media at
a time that prevents one from scooping the other. However, if
a newspaper reporter develops a story on his own, there is no
obligation for the superintendent to inform the radio reporter
of the lead in advance. It is to be assumed that the radio reporter had the same opportunity to uncover the story.

USE THE RIGHT MEDIUM FOR THE RIGHT PURPOSE

The superintendent must also recognize the peculiar merits
of competitive channels of communication for stories. Some
stories, enriched with photographs, lend themselves naturally
to newspaper exploitation, while radio and television have the
obvious advantage in public relations activities involving
sound. The administrator does not have to be fair here, nor
will one medium object to the utilization of the other for its
particular advantages as long as the opportunities do not favor
one consistently.

The popularity of television has caused school personnel to
reappraise the value of radio for public relations purposes.
Even radio management admit that they have had to revise
their concepts of what function they can now serve best. Tele-

vision has by no means replaced radio as an advertising or entertaining medium. In fact, commercial statistics show that there were more radio sets sold in 1956 than in any previous year of production. The difference lies in the time of day that the mass of the listening audience allocates to radio. Radio broadcasters still enjoy great numbers of listeners in the automobile, on the beach, around the house when mothers are doing work that involves their eyes, and for local news. However, school personnel can no longer count on attracting sizable radio audiences in the evening, which was formerly the most sought-after time. They must answer honestly, "Who would intentionally tune in on a mediocre school production when a professional television program is available?"

If it is important to get across a particular message via radio, the superintendent will do well to consider the repetitive spot announcement.

WELL-WRITTEN BROCHURES ARE THE BEST FORMAL PUBLIC RELATIONS DEVICE

Simple, well-written brochures sent home with pupils are apt to constitute the best means of keeping parents informed of how the school is doing what. The "take-home" leaflets issued with report cards, which explain briefly how reading is taught, or what the art program attempts to accomplish, or the place of sports in education, are excellent good will devices.

One of the important requirements in the preparation of these brochures is to avoid the appearance of costly, ostentatious productions. The current fad of publishing handsome leaflets and annual reports has resulted in some top-grade publications that any industry would be proud to have originated. For the sake of creating favorable public attitudes, however, there is a vital difference between an attractive, readable publication and a pretentious extravaganza. Superintendents need to remember the first essential step for any successful writer— to put himself in the place of the reader. What is the reader's reaction to a glamorous publication from the school?

Perhaps the most difficult obstacle in the preparation of a school informational organ is the acquiring of a style to attract adult readers. Teachers, the best educated class of people in a community, are generally the poorest writers for reaching the average layman. They cannot shed their pedagogical terminology, their factual research approach, or their textbook philosophy that is so foreign to the man in the street. At this point, of course, a publicity specialist could have value. However, in any school system there are persons who have the necessary skill for composing readable copy, and a wise superintendent will utilize those talents.

DO ENOUGH PUBLIC RELATIONS ACTIVITIES— BUT NOT TOO MUCH

The successful superintendent must find an acceptable path between tthe psychologically extreme reactions to the extent and frequency of school public relations efforts. It can be overdone. One able city superintendent who is adept and aggressive with the activity would hear this comment if he were tuned in to his community, "He's more concerned with public relations than with the education of our children."

On the other hand, people read and remember only those items in which they are interested at the moment. In one community where the superintendent was unusually skilled in producing informational materials there had been distributed during a two-year period considerable data on the school's science program. A good "take-home" leaflet had been developed, several articles with accompanying pictures had appeared in the newspaper, a newly formed science club in the high school had received considerable local attention with its activities and use of community resources, and proper releases had been made regarding the scientific achievements of graduates in college and industry. However, when the nation became upset over Russia's satellite, there was a storm of inquiry into the local school's science program. After investigation, and with further dissemination of data, the citizens quieted down, but the question was raised over and over again, "Why didn't you tell us about our excellent science program?"

This true incident also illustrates the importance of timing in the release of information. It suggests further that it never hurts to put one's good foot forward repeatedly.

CITIZENS COMMITTEES ARE VALUABLE FOR KEEPING COMMUNITY CROSS-SECTIONS INFORMED

A more recent device for keeping the public informed on school matters is the citizens' committee. As long as such organizations are viewed with that limited purpose in mind, they can be of considerable value. It is difficult, though, to stir enough interest for holding together very long a group of busy citizens when the informational objective alone is pursued. Eventually, members will want to sink their teeth into a problem and do something about it, and in so doing may usurp the proper function of a board of education or superintendent. At this juncture a citizens' committee can become more of a liability than an asset. As a means of reaching wide segments of the community with information direct from the horse's mouth, or of merely soliciting advice from a wider representation than the normal channels which are available to the superintendent and board, citizens' committees are meritorious.

ENCOURAGE ATTENDANCE AT BOARD MEETINGS FOR PUBLIC RELATIONS BENEFITS

Encouraging public attendance at board meetings is another valuable public relations activity. Granted, not many citizens are sufficiently interested to appear at a board meeting unless there is before them an issue of personal concern. Some boards make it easier for people to attend by conducting their meetings in various school buildings around the city. Actually, a superintendent can test with some degree of reliability the school's Hooper rating in the community by the attendance at board meetings. If few people appear, especially after recurring invitations, he can be assured that most of the people have confidence in his and the board's judgment. Showing a willingness to have all school matters opened to the public is the best way to cure suspicion.

To Answer, or Not to Answer
Attacks on Education

Every superintendent will face on occasion a decision as to the feasibility of answering criticism of the schools. His conclusion will be influenced by weighing the tendency for people to believe what they hear and read, against the power of time to heal all wounds and faith in the common sense of people. In one community the superintendent chose to ignore last-minute, below-the-belt accusations from the opposition to a proposed bond issue. He concluded that it was below his dignity to stoop to the same tactics in answering the attacks, and he relied upon his faith in people to see through the opposition's methods. The bond issue was defeated. At another time in that same community the newspaper reported an exaggerated story about the extent of drinking at a high school dance. The superintendent rushed in with a story of denial, a story that gave the actual facts, and generally praised the character of youth. The common reaction at the bridge table, at the service club luncheon, and in the office was, "The old boy sure tried to cover up for the delinquents, didn't he!"

No one can predict accurately what the public reaction to news will be. However, there are certain knowledges one gains with experience which can help the superintendent in making his decision.

In the first place, it must be recognized that most people like scandal and sensationalism. They will believe what rumors they want to believe. No man, however powerful his personal influence might be, is going to change those facts. Normally, the best tool for combating the scandal rumors that are bound to develop about students is a continual deliberate program of giving public recognition to the commendable activities of youth. Inviting citizens to school affairs to see what actually goes on is another helpful tool.

School people are super sensitive to criticism. They probably suffer more anguish and feel more martyrdom about a "bad press" than any other category of occupationals except politicians and doctors. Just how excited educators become over criticism can be realized from the barrage of angry, monotonous articles in the professional journals that follow every attack on schools, or by observing the agenda of a professional meeting after the attack. We tell each other over and over again how unfair the criticism was and try to bolster our defenses. While this is good for morale purposes, it would be more fruitful if we could evaluate each criticism calmly and objectively to see if it has some degree of merit, and reply to the attack unemotionally if it deserves an answer.

Criticism of public schools stems from assorted motives—publicity seeking, fanaticism, sincere anxieties, urge to reform, private interests, misinformation, and from columnists merely looking for a filler. Educators must distinguish the motive and react accordingly. There exists an obligation to correct erroneous notions which may be abroad in a community. It is possible, however, to arouse more doubt and suspicion by frantic, thunderous denunciations than by respectful aloofness. "Where there's smoke, there's fire," people are apt to remember.

Chancing redundancy for the sake of emphasis, it is repeated that "time heals most problems." If a successful superintendent were to answer honestly how he solved most of the school problems which he has faced in his lifetime, he would have to admit that the passing of time, and not his ability, was his biggest ally. His ability is sometimes demonstrated when he exercises the acuity and patience to let his most loyal associate work for him. This advice is especially pertinent when a reporter uses the "sucker-bait" or "expected denial" type of story in which he can't discover the truth and therefore plants a slight distortion in the hope that someone will deny it with the truth.

Communities, as well as situations, vary in governing the reaction of a superintendent toward poor press releases. There
are communities, and occasional emergencies in any community, in which the majority of the people understand and respect bold, slam-bang tactics. Under these circumstances, a
superintendent cannot hide behind the dignity that usually
shrouds his profession. No superintendent can always refuse to
get his hands dirty. If a community expects garbage-can tactics, the superintendent had better know where garbage is
stored—or else move on to a community with higher standards
of sanitation.

Public Relations in a Nutshell

A summarizing suggestion for public relations: The best
program for public school public relations is so subtle that it
never appears to be one. People are skeptical, even resentful,
toward anyone who is obviously trying to win friends. An ideal
plan would consist of providing the best possible educational
program under capable teachers and administrators, with just
enough overt activity to keep people interested and informed
of what is going on within the schools.

chapter eight

The Little Things That Count

A book dedicated to helping superintendents to be successful would commit an unforgivable sin of omission if it neglected advice on the little things that count. The subjects discussed hereinafter may seem inconsequential and below the dignity of a professional book, and yet, as any public figure knows, people evaluate him as much by his personal attributes and actions as by his technical capabilities, perhaps even more on a local level. Some otherwise able school administrators have joined the casualty list because of their breaches of community mores or of common sense standards of conduct; others have been prevented from joining the ranks of the successful new brand of superintendency through inattention to their family's behavior. A superintendent's house is not his own.

The suggestions offered are modified with the usual reservations that no two communities, superintendents, or their families are identical. A list of do's and don'ts could be endless. It is assumed that an educated man has acquired at least ordinary understanding of society's behavioral expectations; therefore, only those matters will be cited here which have caused the most frequent concern.

Community Relationships

The points have already been made about the importance of the superintendent's public relations and the extent to which he is expected to participate in the community's better projects. This section is concerned with the personal conduct of his community affairs in such a way that it will not detract from his effectiveness as a school administrator.

STAY OUT OF MAIN STREET'S BATTLES

The need for counsel along these lines is manifested by a few known incidents. All four superintendents had one thing in common in addition to poor judgment—they soon looked for new positions; three by virtue of being without jobs and one who beat 'em to the punch. One openly campaigned for the election of a mayor. Another made a public speech in favor of cutting down trees on a beautiful boulevard to make way for a wider street. Still another entered a bitter church feud over whether or not the minister should go. And another served as campaign manager for his favorite school board member.

There are several sound reasons why the superintendent should remain aloof from local issues that disturb emotional stability. First, the public schools constitute the one agency in the community that has absolutely no ax to grind. There is no motive for their perpetuation other than to educate children. This can be the only justification for persons being employed by the board of education, including the superintendent. Therefore, when the superintendent becomes embroiled in other than educational activities he automatically involves the public schools, for few citizens can dissociate in their minds the thought of the superintendent from the thought of the public schools.

Secondly, in keeping the schools free to perform their intended role he must keep himself free from obligation to persons or points of view. He dare not allow himself to be squeezed into the position where allies may take advantage of his friendship, or where oppositional forces of one issue can exert pressure in order that he may regain their good graces on another issue.

It is also unethical for a superintendent to lend the stature that has been built into his office to the support of any cause other than the one it is intended to serve—education.

There is also a realistically personal reason for his avoiding community strife. The stand he takes might be the losing one.

This advice should not be interpreted so narrowly that he must always be a fence-straddler and never stand up to be counted. There are certain community struggles in which he is expected to be in the right corner—the causes of morality, safety, patriotism, and the sanctity of motherhood.

AVOID ENTANGLING ALLIANCES

The sagas of national figures are often spectacularized by their excessive attachments to favorite people, animals, or hobbies, but such has seldom enhanced the respect in which they are held. It is easier, of course, for people to discover the excesses of their local leaders. Many people get their kicks out of making sport of the leisure-time obsessions among their public office holders, creating uncomplimentary nicknames and slogans. The superintendent is most likely to invite such abuse through his exclusive social affiliations with one group or class of people, or through an exaggerated pursuit of recreation that keeps him away from work an unreasonable amount of time.

This does not deny him the joy of close friendships, social or civic pastimes, or recreation. Rather, it is intended to urge that he seek breadth more than depth in his community associations. This is also helpful in his need to create good will in as many circles as possible and to keep in touch with community sentiment regarding education.

DO AS THE ROMANS DO

It is superfluous to caution most superintendents about their social behavior, and still one cannot overlook the number of casualties attributed to their extremes in moral conduct—licentious as well as prudish. Moreover, it is difficult under society's changing moral restrictions to know precisely the limitations a given community prescribes for its community leaders. Boundaries of propriety are confused further by the customs of different communities and the varying habits of groups within a community whose paths the superintendent is likely to cross. It would be convenient to have a single formula to guide all superintendents in this respect, but one can offend as quickly by overbearing intemperance as by libertine rakishness.

There is just one principle which, if used sensibly, can be resurrected for steering superintendents through this dilemma —"when in Rome, do as the Romans do," whether Rome be a community or a segment thereof. Again, for the benefit of the literalist, this does not mean that a superintendent is under compulsion to humor Bacchus, Culbertson, or the Charleston when surrounded by their devotees; but at least he can refrain from aggravating them. Nor does it mandate that he must test his endurance just because the gang does. The maxim can be improved upon by holding high the deeds of the moderate Romans, whatever the gathering.

DRESS THE PART

The housing for some of education's mightiest brain power is supported by bodies draped in slovenly getups. Most of these persons have made their names on college campuses where appearance is not of the essence, and where eccentricity is not only tolerated but fertilized by some in an effort to acquire a trademark. The public is not so patient with the noncomformist, in the matter of dress as well as mannerisms. The educator-superintendent, therefore, must respect the common yardsticks with which citizens measure his brain power.

Women, and the business world, long ago discovered the importance of appearance for successful personal relationships, as have the new brand of superintendents. A little more attention to this apparently insignificant aspect of his impressionistic talents will pay dividends for the superintendent who wants to advance. If his training in this regard has been neglected, there are numerous sources of helpful information: books, articles, his wife, his secretary, or a friendly haberdasher.

A FEW WELL-CHOSEN WORDS

The requirement for the modern superintendent to communicate articulately is so urgent as to make it astonishing that more universities have not insisted upon at least one good course in public speaking in their administrative preparatory programs. Weakness in the ability to speak intelligently, or even grammatically correct English, explains why many able administrators have fallen short of greatness. It scarcely seems necessary to establish the need for the skill; one merely has to reflect upon the fact that approximately 90 per cent of the superintendent's work involves face-to-face relationships. Not only is he responsible for making appropriate administrative decisions, but for selling levies and bond issues, his own ideas, and himself. Today's aggressive administrator will deliver from twenty-five to one hundred public addresses a year, will participate in dozens of small group discussions, and will be called upon to respond with a few pithy remarks an uncountable number of times during the year.

To the superintendent who has already passed the probability of further college training, it is still not too late to develop facility with public speaking. If he is too self-conscious to enroll in the local adult education classes, he can acquire a do-it-yourself textbook and practice on his wife. Overcoming the dread of public oration is little different from combating any other fear—just face it again and again.

The Superintendent's Home and Family

If a superintendent is denied the pleasure of living a normal, uninhibited life at least his family ought to be exempt from this restriction. But such is not their destiny, either. They and their house are part of the glass bowl into which the public stares to appraise the superintendent's effectiveness as an administrator. If the family is unwilling to accept this limitation upon their freedom they should not complain about his failure to progress in the profession. Once they acknowledge this handicap, however, they will discover that the prohibitions are not too throttling; in fact, life can be beautiful.

A few suggestions are offered.

THE WIFE WAS NOT HIRED AS SUPERINTENDENT

Her actions in this regard can literally make or break a superintendent. Her interference, or even influence, in his administrative decisions can be as detrimental to his success as any shortcoming he might possess on his own. Even in those rare instances when the power behind the throne is a more capable administrator than the throne, her ability will pay off only if she permits the illusion that he is the power.

Probably the safest course of action in order to abide by this advice is for the wife to be the most ignorant citizen about school affairs, ostensibly at least. In this way, she has a logical and graceful excuse for dodging probing questions in her social contacts. It requires real talent for a wife to show interest in her husband's work without projecting herself into his decisions.

THE SUPERINTENDENT'S WIFE SHOULD BE MODERATE IN HER TASTES, THOUGHTS, AND ACTIONS, AT LEAST PUBLICLY

Ostentatiousness is rarely in good taste for any respectable woman, but particularly not for the superintendent's wife. If the little lady cannot agree to this standard of living, the husband will probably be wise in selecting another occupation. An acceptable compromise with her urge to splash could be within her home. Even though the superintendent's house, too, is somewhat of a greenhouse, still she is entitled to the privacy inherent in managing a home.

THE WIFE IS GENERALLY EXPECTED TO ASSUME SOME LEADERSHIP ROLE IN COMMUNITY AND SCHOOL AFFAIRS

This is not compulsory, and wives of some of the most able school administrators have managed to avoid the town's activities. Nevertheless, it is a common expectation that the superintendent's wife should contribute a share of her talent and energy to local civic, charity, church, and school extracurriculars, almost to the degree that is expected of him. Here, again, it calls for diplomacy and common sense for the wife to participate in, but not dominate, community affairs to the point of arousing animosities. And a still greater amount of self-control is essential for the loyal wife to refrain from zealous defense of her husband and other school people when criticism is heard at community affairs.

SPECIAL EDUCATION FOR THE SUPERINTENDENT'S CHILDREN

Children of public figures are a special breed in society and deserve a mink-lined nest in the Hereafter. They grow up in the center of the arena and can't possibly perform to the expectations of the audience. If they do something praiseworthy, it's because either they had a better opportunity than other children or else Dad gave them an unearned break. If their deeds slip below par, everyone enjoys it and it is the result of the parents' neglect. It is extremely difficult, if not impossible, for a parent in public life to bring up his children in "normal" patterns. The superintendent's children are no exception; in fact, they are prime examples. It is little wonder so many of this special breed of society's handicapped youngsters turn sour.

Fortunately, well-trained educators have a better background for coping with the situation. They are, at least, aware of the problems facing their children and of child growth principles. The following suggestions are offered to assist the superintendent further in this respect.

When the child is of school age, the superintendent should go out of his way to let the teachers know that he expects no

favoritism for his offspring and that he would appreciate their
helping him to provide as normal experiences as possible. At
no time should he use his child as a check on the teacher. He
must even be cautious in asking his child the usual parental
questions, "What did you learn in school today?" or "How did
things go today?" or "How do you like your teacher?" Small
children, especially, are apt to repeat their conversations with
Daddy in the presence of the teacher, who might misinterpret
the motive behind the questions.

The superintendent must resist the natural parental tendency to evaluate the teacher or the entire school in terms of his
own child's experiences. Further, he dare not shove his child
into the limelight, in the community as well as in the school.
The aggressive youngster of a public figure is usually in for a
rougher go from his peers than one who demonstrates mod-
esty. On the other hand, the superintendent's child need not be
discouraged from developing special talents. Many children of
superintendents have managed to achieve outstanding records
as scholars, athletes, musicians, and dramatists without feeling
undue pressure from the crowd. The determining factor between accomplishing these feats with or without criticism
seems to be the matter of whether there is any semblance of
the child having capitalized on his father's position.

BUY THE RIGHT HOUSE

Any citizen, even to include a superintendent of schools, has
the American right to live where he chooses according to his
station, in the type of home he prefers, and to rent or buy his
home if he wishes. But to exercise a right can constitute a
wrong. The shrewd superintendent is aware of his peculiar
status in the community as well as he is of human reactions to
his actions.

Discounting the financial aspects of deciding upon a home,
the superintendent in tune with lay sensitivities will buy rather
than rent. By renting he will be exposing himself needlessly to
barbs from other taxpayers when he leads a campaign for in-

creased school taxes. Moreover, purchasing a home meets with the American respect for stability as a member of the community. It also makes the real estate board happy.

Furthermore, building up an equity in a home through time payments is one way the superintendent can force himself to save. It might even profit him to build a new house since today's superintendent should be familiar with construction materials and techniques in order to perform well his professional responsibilities.

Choosing a location is a decision that should not be taken lightly. In a new community the superintendent should delay long enough to get the feel of the community. For prestige reasons he ought not to locate in a blighted section of town. For common sense reasons he should not locate in the most exclusive section. He probably can't afford it, anyhow. The middle upper class region is unquestionably the ideal. The importance of selecting the site within the taxing district where he is employed hardly needs emphasizing.

WATCH THAT BUDGET

Among the little things that count in the success of school administrators there is probably none that has put them in more hot water than carelessness with personal finances. There are still some superintendents who are much better educators than they are businessmen. Administrative positions have been lost through such inexcusable acts as failure to pay housekeeping bills while purchasing extravagant automobiles, clothing, and vacation trips; living beyond income; or moving away with a substantial debt unpaid. Forgiveness to such superintendents can be extended only in the event of a sudden and unavoidable serious misfortune which depleted the family savings.

Budgeting of personal income is a must. A superintendent who can't plan and execute a family budget adequately can scarcely be entrusted with a public budget. Moreover, a salaried man has easier budgeting problems than one without a regular fixed income. Pursuing rigorously a plan of setting aside just 10 per cent of his income for savings over a normal lifetime will build up a tidy nest egg.

Nearly all school employees today automatically enjoy favorable provisions for retirement. In most instances, however, a school person would want to supplement this with some form of insurance plan. Many schools also provide opportunities for employees to obtain at reasonable cost protection against extended illness or permanent disability. The one area left uncovered by numerous school officials, however, is the protection for the family against the breadwinner's death at an early age. Without inviting argument from insurance representatives, a declining type of term insurance is a good method for filling this gap. Such a plan would yield a large amount to his beneficiaries if he should die young, but the benefits are reduced gradually over the years as he approaches the time when his full retirement or life insurance could handle the financial needs of his family.

If the "average" superintendent has the "average" amount of success, fortune, and financial acumen, he will arrive at the point where he has a small surplus of money which he would like to put to work for him. The opportunities are unlimited. Whether he invests in real estate, securities, or a business will depend primarily upon his natural interests and upon his predilections for risk or security. Arguments can be advanced for any kind of investment, but a plug is inserted here for stocks and bonds if for no other reason than to enhance his knowledge in an area with which the modern superintendent ought to have familiarity. It can also constitute an interesting hobby. If a superintendent chooses this form of diversity, he should be cautioned about becoming excessively enthusiastic and greedy to the point of serious financial loss, about spending official time in watching the ticker tape, and about discussing his pastime publicly. Taxpayers aren't pleased with the thought that they're paying their public officials enough to permit investments, too.

Invading the sphere of debate again, family financial author-ities for persons of moderate means advise that a general plan for savings and investments would entail savings, protection for the family, security, and a small amount of risk. The superintendent should first look at the long picture and then to immediate gain. In other words, he should protect himself and his family as he progresses, build for retirement, set aside for emergency needs, and then play with the remainder—if any.

This particular counseling section would be incomplete without a warning to superintendents about being too frugal. There is a difference between economical financial management and niggardly habits. Superintendents of the latter variety do little for the prestige of the profession or for their own progress.

For Health's Sake—Keep Healthy

For most people who work under pressure, the greatest threat to continued success is the body's reluctance to keep pace with drive and ambition. Unless executives observe elementary school physiology rules they are prone to push themselves beyond the durability of their mechanical make-up. The advice submitted here is no more than that given by a General Practitioner to any man who works primarily with his brain, but is necessary to include in a book of this nature since dedicated, conscientious superintendents don't take the time to read it elsewhere.

Have a thorough physical examination at least annually, twice a year is wiser. Many of the body strings that wear out can snap without serving advance notice. Most men would rather suffer illness than to go to a doctor when they're well. A superintendent should heed the call of the spouse when she prods him into a visit to the clinic.

Take that vacation; school will keep. As the American Association of School Administrators survey revealed, few superintendents take the vacation time to which they are entitled, some none at all. The worry-bug frets about having everything ship shape for the opening of school, about the system degenerating in his absence, about being out of reach in case of emergency, about taxpayers wondering if they're getting their money's worth. It can only be concluded that such overly conscientious superintendents are insecure or poor managers.

Also, executives should attend some conventions for the purpose of relaxation even if the programs are not productive of great wisdom.

The full week-ends and frequent holidays available to school personnel are one of the profession's strongest selling points, and the superintendent should not completely deny himself the prerogative. A quick change of environment is an ideal stimulant for clearer thinking and desirable attitudes.

Don't take work home every night—for the same reasons. Furthermore, it isn't fair to the family. More and more industries are accusing their executives of inefficiency if they can't complete their work during office hours.

Develop a hobby that diverts mental processes from school problems. An ideal hobby for a school superintendent would permit constructive physical exercise, sufficient interest to enforce forgetting of daily educational matters, one that can be picked up or dropped to fit the uncertain schedule of a school administrator, that allows some inclusion of the family, that is not extremely expensive, and possibly one that even promises a financial return.

Develop and maintain a sense of humor—for health's sake as well as an aid to professional effectiveness. No other single quality is as valuable in getting a superintendent through his normal day of trivialities, unpleasantness, and tension. Too many superintendents deny themselves the luxury—to be sure, a necessity—of a sense of humor because of a peculiar concept of reserve about the position, or because of being just dull personalities. To be able to see the funny side of situations, or the double meanings in comments, is also a handy device for relaxing a tense audience in order that a superintendent might advance through barriers to win a point.

chapter nine

Have Debts; Will Travel

Since it is impossible to underwrite any advice on how to secure a superintendency position, this chapter will offer it with allowances for that limitation in mind. From years of personal experience, as well as from opinions of other superintendents, it is possible to arrive at only one bonded conclusion on the matter—there is no consistent pattern by which superintendents are selected. Almost any veteran will verify that he seldom got the jobs he sincerely wanted and for which he was ideally suited; the ones he least expected he won. Textbooks and professional journals are pregnant with recommended procedures which one should follow in seeking an administrative appointment. There's probably no harm in heeding the advice; it might even work sometime.

Several true situations are recited below as proof of the disorganized manner of selecting superintendents.

A thirty-two-year-old administrator, whose appearance indicated a mere twenty-five, was turned down for a position because he was too young. A friend of twenty-nine with heavy beard and thick-rimmed glasses applied for the same job and got it. Since this had already happened too often to the youthful-appearing superintendent, he resolved to do something about it when a better position came along soon afterward. He appeared before the next board of education garbed in blue serge, wearing a pair of ten-cent store glasses, and with chalk dust sprinkled artfully in his hair. He got the job.

Another superintendent received his first appointment

165

mainly on the condition that he didn't smoke. For his latest appointment, the city superintendency which he presently holds, he was interviewed by the employing board in a cocktail lounge.

Some boards like to impress their constituency with the thoroughness with which they searched for a new superintendent, although they may have made their decision at the time the vacancy was announced. Recently a superintendent from the Far West received the notice of a vacancy in one of the more promising eastern cities. The invitation to apply carried not only the customary compliment that he had been highly recommended for the position but also a commendable statement of criteria for applicants. He was so inspirited with the school system and with the professional tone used by the board in undertaking the task of hiring a new superintendent that he spent many hours in completing the application. He also exerted effort in composing his accompanying letter to indicate his sincerity in wanting to become affiliated with a community of that stature. Some weeks later he learned the facts. About ninety candidates had been invited to apply; some twenty were called in for interviews. The board appointed their assistant superintendent, as they had agreed among themselves to do from the beginning.

Occasionally a board will entrust the job of finding a new superintendent, the most important function it has to perform, to the departing superintendent. One superintendent recently received this telephone call from the superintendent of a Chicago suburb, "I'm leaving for a better position and am flying through your state tomorrow interviewing prospective candidates. My plane has a layover in your city and since you've been recommended as my successor, could you meet me at the airport for an interview?" The prospective applicant's decision was prompt and forthright, "I am interested in a better position, but not with any school board that would permit the present superintendent to fly about the country on the taxpayers' money to name his own successor."

A few years ago a superintendent resigned his position in a moment of extreme irritation with this headlined causticism, "There must be an easier way to earn a living." He was just finishing the first year of a five-year contract. Immediately the board interviewed candidates and decided upon his successor who, thereupon, resigned his former position.

Before the board took official action on either the resignation or the new appointment, their present superintendent, with ulcers under control, decided he had acted too hastily. He told the board he had changed his mind and didn't want to resign. Answered the board, "Sorry, we've already filled the position." He replied, "Sorry, you can't. Although I submitted my resignation in writing, you never officially accepted it."

And he was right. The law in that state provides that no resignation is effective until the board takes official action in a regularly called session. He served out his remaining four years and entered private business. The other fellow went into college teaching—probably teaching school law.

Superintendents have been hired without ever meeting the board of education members. A board should receive credentials and recommendations, but that's scarcely enough.

Other boards go to the opposite extreme, arranging for candidates to meet nearly everyone in the community but the chimney sweep. The current rage for having candidates interviewed by faculty and/or citizen representatives has much in its favor. A superintendent ought to be able to get along with the faculty and community. Moreover, the approach is in tune with the democratic philosophy in that it allows these groups to think they are sharing in the selection of the boss. There are known instances, however, when the recommendations of these groups are given no more consideration than the vote of a prospective child as to who his parents ought to be. It would be intriguing to know how the board explains it to its committees when the latter's recommendee is not tapped for the job. The board should delegate the responsibility completely or else go it alone. Under no circumstances should the technique be employed to tease the staff or citizens into a false sense of community cooperation. In fact, the legality of the practice might be questioned if the committee is given any serious responsibility since the law holds the board of education responsible for hiring a superintendent.

It is still rather common practice to employ superintendents on a "What'll you come for?" basis. The law of supply and demand has currently discouraged the technique to a degree. Back in depression days, when the availability of applicants far exceeded the opportunities, a board would narrow the choice down to three or five top prospects, and then award the position to the man who would come for the least salary. Many professional friendships were ruined by candidates' underbidding one another. Competitive bidding still prevails with a slightly different twist. Usually boards establish a salary range within which they hope to catch a fish. At times they may have to go higher than the predetermined maximum in order to lure a particularly appetizing prospect. On the other hand, it is likely they will find adequate possibilities who will be satisfied with the range; and if they can secure one for $8,000 who seems "almost as good" as the one with a $10,000 label, they are prone to save $2,000 for the taxpayers.

One superintendent reports that he was appointed to his position primarily because he was a war veteran; another because he had had no military experience; another because of his business experience before entering the educational profession; one because he had a doctoral degree, and another because that particular board wanted no part of a man with advanced degrees; one because of his enrapturing wife, another because he was single, and still another because he had the fewest school-age children in a system whose buildings were already overcrowded; one because of his Phi Beta Kappa achievement, and another because his college academic grades were not straight A's; one because of his lengthy participation in PTA affairs, and another because he had permitted no PTA's in his previous assignment; one because he had remained in one administrative post for fifteen years, and another because he had advanced six times within a twelve-year period.

WHAT IS THE CRITERION FOR SELECTION? YOU NAME IT!

Employment history of superintendents abounds with such examples; all of which prove nothing more than the text of this chapter, viz., there is no reliable pattern by which superintendents are chosen. The decision to hire may be made at a chamber of commerce convention as the board member from one city chats at a dinner with a club member from another district; by running a police MO in the candidate's community, by taking the placement officer's word that he's a good man; by interview; by employing a consultant to guide the board's decision; by merely examining credentials; or by boosting someone already in the system.

The cardinal factor which determines why a particular prospect is employed, or rejected, may be his dress, mannerisms, size, age, grammar, voice, wife, college record, credit rating, military record, service club, or dirty fingernails; his philosophy toward labor, big business, alcohol, religion, sex, athletics, the free enterprise system, the gifted child, phonetics, individual differences, high school fraternities, Truman, integration, the Civil War, or any other conceivable reason that could be labeled a reason.

Trends in Employment Practices

A few recognizable trends and techniques are beginning to take shape and merit attention. For example, *there has been an increasing tendency for boards to invite universities to nominate candidates*. The universities approached usually include the larger ones, those in the area, and the ones from which board members graduated. The practice has promising possibilities. At least an alert college placement office keeps track of its successful graduates, and it generally makes a sincere effort to recommend candidates who not only have a reasonable chance of satisfying the board but also of landing the job. They are compelled to do this in order to get repeat business. Although college placement offices are not in it for a profit, the university itself is on trial.

It is the desire to impress the dean, or to beat competition, that occasionally leads placement officers into overzealous practices. Some officers will find a "suitable" candidate among their alumni for every good job, even if they have to close their eyes to some minor shortcomings. Others will hop a plane to a plum position, armed with a satchel of credentials, and try to sew up the appointment before competing colleges have made their play. The White Slave Act does not cover all aspects of human auction.

Some placement enthusiasts gain their satisfactions from life by playing the "falling domino" game, sometimes referred to as the "progressive party" technique—not to be confused with progressive education. The object of the game is to land a big job and then fill the resulting vacancy by another alumnus, who creates an opportunity for a third alumnus, and so on. Sometimes the game lasts from the first vacancy in March until the last post is filled in late August, the lucky player always having the jump on competition because he knows first where the next vacancy will occur. An outside domino watches the play from the sidelines, waiting for the right vacancy to appear for which he considers himself eligible, and then attempts to jump into the line. The game could be endless but is usually called when school has to start in September. There is undoubtedly a good master's thesis in discovering what happens to the last lowly vacancy.

Presenting a doctoral degree is becoming increasingly important in order to establish eligibility for the better positions. Many boards are saying, "Doctorate preferred"; a few insist on it. The former is a more desirable procedure inasmuch as a board may have to compromise its specifications after searching among the few doctorates yet available. A Master's degree is almost an essential for any worthwhile administrative post. It is a hopeful sign that more and more boards are recognizing that the superintendency is a distinct profession requiring specialized training.

There is also a tendency today for an employing board to look beyond local borders, county and state, for the next superintendent. For the larger city systems, of course, it is virtually obligatory; but even the medium-sized cities are scouring the country for prospects. Home-state pride is still prevalent and is not to be underrated by a superintendent as a factor in deciding where to search for a position. Nevertheless, the inclination to take a look at least past state boundary lines is growing.

A concomitant trend is to appoint an outsider rather than to elevate from within. The human reaction to "grass being greener on the other side of the fence" drives many boards to overlook potentialities existing within the staff. Local citizens are ofttimes too close to the staff members for objective evaluations. Opposition to this practice is heard from the staff who resent the oversight, from those who fear that the new broom may sweep too clean, and from those who know there will be a year's lull in progress while the new man gets the lay of the land. It is probably a safe assumption, however, that the school system generally profits with a new personality, a fresh approach, and the avoidance of inbreeding.

Similarly, *the most traveled path of advancement for superintendents is from smaller systems to larger ones.* In seeking a superintendent, boards want a man who is a superintendent now. Rarely do they take seriously the application of a college student or college teacher, of an assistant superintendent in a larger system, or of an educator presently employed in a state department of education, or from someone in an occupation other than education. Superintendents working in larger or wealthier school districts than the one seeking a replacement rule themselves out of consideration by their higher salaries. The only source for applicants, therefore, are the superintendents in the slightly smaller or poorer school districts. Occasionally, a board thinks there is something distinctly attractive about its schools or community that will interest superintendents in the same population or income bracket. They are disillusioned to learn that superintendents change jobs for the same reason that other occupationals do—more money.

The search for younger men goes on in educational administrative circles in the same manner as it does in industry. The former practice of promoting the oldest and most experienced teacher to the superintendent's post has virtually disappeared in favor of the young professionally trained specialist. It is an accepted maxim among superintendents that wherever a man is serving at age forty-eight, there he will finish his days. Boards are rarely interested in any candidate over forty-five; the specifications frequently are from thirty-five to forty-five. This fact works to the detriment of both the school system and the men in the profession. The fact that a superintendent can't improve his position after that age means that the present school system is saddled with him until he retires. Most boards are sufficiently charitable that they will not take action to remove an older superintendent for anything short of criminal conduct, so the school system patiently bides his retirement. Witness the fact that the newspaper accounts of a retiring superintendent nearly always refer to "his past twenty or more years in the system." Then the search begins anew for the forty-year-old man who is considered sufficiently mature and experienced to handle the job but fancied as being too senile if he's a day older.

There is also an increasing tendency for boards to conduct a thorough search in a prospect's previous communities before deciding to appoint him. This has always been the best technique for determining potential success. Unfortunately, the process takes board members' time and a piece of their change, with the result that boards are inclined to rely upon written recommendations, interviews, and credentials. Checking in just one previous assignment may not reveal all the necessary information. A man can have good or poor success in one system contrary to his experience in several others. Wide sampling in the community is also advisable for the same reason. The opinions of one or two individuals could be misleading. If a board uncovers a general attitude of "I hope you don't take him from us" existing among teachers, board members, the editor of the newspaper, PTA officer, chamber of commerce secretary, a banker, a judge, the credit bureau, and the minister, it can be reasonably sure it would be wise to take him. A personal investigation of this nature can put the candidate in an embarrassing position in case he isn't chosen, so the inquiring pollsters owe it to the man to be discreet and ethical.

The shrewd and ethical superintendent will also inform his own board if he is considering another position. No board member likes to be caught short with the prospect of having to seek another chief executive. To apply for another job without informing one's present board is as discourteous as a husband flirting with another man's wife without his own wife's knowledge—if not as dangerous.

While it is difficult to substantiate with concrete evidence, there appear to be enough known cases to consider it a trend that *boards more and more in selecting a superintendent are looking "at the man" rather than at his degrees, experience, age, or any other factor alone.* The evidence is found in the numerous selections which defy all trends and predictions of what would seem to be a logical choice. It is the unknown ingredient which accounts for the conclusion that there are few patterns for selecting superintendents. It is also the reason why little advice can be given prospective superintendents that will help their cause in applying. No one can be assured what particular trait might strike the fancy of a dominant board member on a given evening. It is the reason why there are so many candidates for any vacancy—who knows in what direction the magic wand might point?

Interviewing Techniques

Advice is bountiful on how one might land almost any type of job except a public school superintendency. Let this be the first, therefore, with the customary reservation that one can only generalize about the interviewing techniques that might work. No warranty accompanies these suggestions, but they have been fruitful for many superintendents.

A candidate should learn something about the board members and the school-community problems before the interview. Going into that meeting cold is the mistake *fatale*. No two schools have identical problems, and no two boards have the same major concerns. A candidate may have landed his present job because of his faith in homogeneous grouping, but this board may be on a democratic binge. Every member will have a particular whim about which he is presently excited. These should be discovered before the interview, and the former superintendent is the best source for this intimate information.

One of the most effective techniques is for the applicant to take into the interview five copies (or as many as there are board members) of the statistics covering his experience, training, and personal data, with a picture attached. Inevitably, an early question will be, "Tell us something about yourself and your experience." That is the candidate's cue to extract the copies from his briefcase casually and say something like, "I thought you might be interested in my history, and perhaps this will save you some time." They'll like that because they've probably already interviewed four other candidates during the evening, and they're hoping they can be home in time for the fights. It leaves the impression that the prospect is a good organizer and gives him time to analyze their characters. It is important to learn as early as possible in the interview which board member is the stinker.

This technique is also helpful with shy board members who

worry more about asking an intelligent question than getting an intelligent answer. Be sure the picture is attached to the data sheet and left with them, for after they've combed through seventy-five applications and interviewed twenty-five candidates, faces and facts begin fading into a mass of bespeckled unknowns. The photo will help them remember who that good organizer was.

It is especially important to know everything possible about a school's and a community's problems before saying "yes" if the board seems intensely interested in a candidate. The serious headaches seldom come out in the interviews. When board members enthusiastically want a man, they are the best salesmen for the community the chamber of commerce has— good staff, interested parents, no pressures, economical housing, plenty of operating money, and roses here, roses there. It is just as necessary for a candidate to run his personal survey in the new board's community as vice versa. If the picture is painted Shangri-La bright, the superintendent should start opening closet doors. Besides, it won't hurt to keep the board sweating a few days about his decision. That way they'll think they got a better bargain.

During the interview a candidate should speak confidently, and authoritatively, and smile frequently. Some men have mastered the art of overawing an audience with a straightforward manner even when they aren't sure of their ground. There are times to admit one's ignorance, but a board will not respond favorably to many replies of "I don't know the answer to that question." Chances are they won't know the right answer either, and businessmen are impressed with the positive approach.

Manage to flatter artfully the feminine member of the board. Women haven't changed since Adam charmed Eve. A personal compliment is much more interesting to her than how the budget is planned, which she won't understand anyhow.

A candidate should have a few carefully selected and pertinent questions ready to bring up before the board. This helps during a lull in the inquisition, and also indicates that he is hep to the situation. "Carefully selected" needs to be underscored so that he will not ask embarrassing questions which won't help his popularity at all. One superintendent innocently asked an interviewing board if it had settled a ticklish problem that had received state-wide notoriety. He did not know that the board was split on the issue and that he had opened a tender wound they were trying to forget. He didn't get that appointment. The candidate should have the questions in mind and not written out. Pulling out a list might lead them to think he's a systematic, detailed administrator incapable of "thinking big," or perhaps that he is just too cockeyed inquisitive.

Under no circumstances should a candidate become so anxious for a job that he makes commitments which he cannot fulfill. Some superintendents have made that mistake, a natural one, to be sure, in the pressure of the final drive for a plum position, but much to their longtime regrets. Wild promises might land one position, but it could be the last. Board members don't forget the statements and promises made in an interview. They have the advantage over a candidate by virtue of numbers alone. If each board member asked but three questions, they would have little difficulty recalling the answers, but the interviewee must remember how he answered fifteen questions. One of the best investments a board can make, for the benefit of both parties concerned, is a tape recording of the interview.

Know when to stop talking. Either through a sense of self-importance, or a sincere desire to discuss educational matters, some candidates muff the ball by holding forth too long. It is difficult in a short interview for a board member to know which was the motive for the lengthy discourse, so the odds favor his appraising the prospect as "Too windy; on to the next candidate."

There is also a genuine talent in avoiding the extremes of appearing either overanxious or blasé about the job. Throughout the employment process the successful candidate will manage to create the illusion that he is going to be hard to get. He must appear interested or the board will not bother with him. On the other hand, he must let them think they are getting the breaks in the negotiations and that they are going after him. It is a fascinating race for the driver's seat, and the party who gets there first will drive the winning horse. Superintendents can profit from a study of how effectively good salesmen employ this technique.

Advancement Techniques

There is no better way to advance in the profession, if one is not related to the management, then by simply doing a good job. However, some conscientious persons have worked so assiduously at building an excellent school program that they didn't take the time to publicize their success or to promote their interest in advancement. There are some techniques which the ambitious superintendent may use to help his cause along.

For instance, he should take an active role in some regional, state, or national educational organization. That not only impresses board members but one never knows what an incidental acquaintance can do for him.

For the same reason he should write an occasional article for the professional journals.

For the same reason he should be more than a passive member in a service club, a church, and some other selected local organization.

He should keep his name on the active list at his university placement office and keep in touch with that office. It is still the best bet for leads on openings. Anyone who has to pay a fee for the services of private placement offices today is desperate. If desperate, go ahead and pay the fee.

If one's sole objective is to advance in the profession, he

should apply for every job that is better than the one he now holds. It only betters his odds. One acquaintance regularly threw his hat in the ring fifty times a year. That was par for the course, but one year he made eighty-six. He reasoned that that many boards couldn't find him objectionable. It was never confirmed if he made a substantial contribution to the education of children, but he did advance. He never slowed down until a heart attack ended a youthful career.

It is usually a waste of time to apply for the top positions in the larger cities; they go looking for candidates. Boards are ofttimes suspicious of unsolicited applications, and they derive considerable satisfaction from thinking that they have "uncovered" the ideal man. If a candidate cannot wait for the invitation, he should get someone to recommend him rather than plunging in blindly. If he can't find a contact, and has the time to kill on reckless speculation, he might go ahead and plunge. Lightning could strike, and as already indicated, there are no absolute rules for the game.

Some professionals have improved their opportunities for advancement by capitalizing on the still prevalent notion that an eastern or Ivy College affiliation gives a person some magical advantage over an unwashed graduate of an "ordinary" university. A half century ago the exclusive aroma clung to the person who had acquired some training abroad. Today there are many persons west of the Alleghenies and south of the Mason-Dixon who have transferred that reputation to eastern colleges. For this reason some superintendents have taken a course or two there in order to include it in their credentials. It helps in some localities.

In order to advance, a superintendent and his family must be willing to leave their present environment. After he has progressed so far in one area, the opportunities lie elsewhere in the nation. Some superintendents have lost out in the struggle to the top because of a particularly enchanting house. It has been suggested that buying a house is a mistake for a young superintendent who wants "to go places." Other superintendents become so attached to friends in a community that they can't tear themselves away, ignoring the obvious fact that every community has some nice people. A superintendent must make the decision early in his career whether to advance or to make a permanent home in a community. There are merits to each viewpoint, but he can't have both. There is no way possible for a superintendent to advance professionally within a community.

How Long To Remain in One Assignment

A recurring question that perturbs superintendents in their years of advancement pertains to the optimum duration of service in a community. In reflecting upon their careers, older superintendents are heard to opine, "If I hadn't stayed so long in Yville," or "If I hadn't moved so often," followed by the implication that they would have gone further. As in other aspects of school administration, one can never be sure about the optimum tenure. The answer also depends upon whether one is thinking in terms of the welfare of the superintendent or of education.

The only certain conclusion is, again, that one should avoid the extremes. For one with ambitions to go far, ten to fifteen years in one assignment will put him beyond the eligible age limit for getting there. Contrariwise, a man who moves every year or two over a period of time will arouse suspicion as to his ability to hold a job. Also, an employing board will wonder how long he will stay with them. However, some counselors on the subject have said that as long as each move is to a better position, it doesn't make any difference how rapidly he jumps.

A capable superintendent is going to advance regardless of the accompanying circumstances. A man cannot be blamed for improving his status. But he certainly has an obligation to the boards and communities that give him the opportunities to advance.

Let us assume it normally requires a year for a superintendent to become sufficiently acquainted with a new situation to be able to make sound judgments and recommendations for the improvement of education. The second year he is ready to develop his ideas, recognizing that it could be disastrous to effect change too rapidly. Perhaps he has done enough for now, but it is not unreasonable to expect him to see his changes through to solid footing. Neither is it too much to ask that he allow time for the evaluation process to occur. It isn't fair, ethical, or humane to let the burden of his misfires fall upon the shoulders of his successor. He can make his own.

In making the decision as to how long one should remain, the superintendent is also caught between two conflicting admonishments: "There will always be opportunities to advance," and "You must take advantage of opportunity when it knocks." It is true that a superintendent has no control over the availability of enticing vacancies. They usually come when he least expects or wants them. Therefore, a superintendent cannot let his conscience disturb him over leaving before his contractual obligations have been fulfilled.

In view of these controversial factors, it is logical to conclude that a minimum tenure in one community should be three to five years. A wise rule of the thumb: don't leave until after you have received the second contract.

chapter ten

Personal Qualities for Successful Superintending; Including Self-Administering Aptitude-Interest Test

The profession of superintendency has now matured to the point where it is possible to analyze the traits of successful practitioners and arrive at reasonably reliable conclusions as to the ingredients required to repeat the achievement. Despite the kaleidoscopic nature of the work and the wide range of abilities men bring to the job, there are still recognizable characteristics common to the majority of successful superintendents. It is the nature of these men that must constitute the basis for predicting success for apprentices in the trade.

In an effort to help a prospective superintendent determine his potential for superintendency insofar as his predispositions are concerned, the following test is submitted. The approach for this determination is through self-analysis.

A warning should be sounded at the outset regarding the limitations of this test. No measuring device has yet been developed, nor is there likely to be, that will approach absolute predictability. Not until science, medicine, psychology, and perhaps religion, combine to provide complete understanding of human behavior will such an ideal be reached. There are too many exceptions to existing aptitude or interest tests to rely upon them with assurance. The best one can conclude from their use is that since people possessing certain qualities have been successful in a given occupation more than have

181

people lacking those qualities, a candidate who demonstrates the desired qualities has better than a fifty-fifty chance of being successful in that field. It is with this qualifying factor in mind that the aptitude and interest test for superintendency is recommended.

For the purpose of this test, success was defined as having served in the capacity of school superintendent for more than ten years and having steadily moved into some of the most sizable and remunerative positions. The definition has assiduously avoided including men who are known to have progressed through happenstance or in defiance of the more frequent appearing qualities that lead to top positions. In using the test to date with successful superintendents as thus defined, there has been a remarkably high similarity of results.

It is recommended that the student complete the test before reading further in this chapter. It is a self-administering device and has value only if the person is seeking honest appraisal of his own nature for possible enjoyment and success in superintendency.

APTITUDE-INTEREST TEST FOR SUPERINTENDENCY
INSTRUCTIONS

After each question, check the *one* answer that best indicates your preference, recommended action, or opinion. Do not omit any items. If the allowed answers do not correspond exactly with your preference or desired course of action under the situation, answer the question anyhow, indicating your one preference among the answers provided. Although some questions may call for deliberation before answering, normally you are urged not to dwell on the matter excessively but to check the answer that appears to you as the best immediate response.

If the test is to have any value at all, the questions must be answered honestly. Do not look at the qualities being measured until after you have finished the test. In some instances you can guess at the "right" answer in terms of what you think the examiner might want you to reply. There is no examiner for this test. You will grade your own test, and no one needs to know your responses. Therefore, a dishonest answer will serve only to deceive yourself.

1. Do you experience such a strong curiosity about a new model of car, boat, gun, or other luxury of your interest that you will "go out of your way" to see it?   Yes_____ No_____

2. Is the desire so strong to be among the first to own that new product that you will ofttimes sacrifice your budget in order to buy it?   Yes_____ No_____

3. If you, as a superintendent, received an anonymous letter criticizing you for a decision you made, would you (a) throw it away (b) show it to the board of education, or (c) put it in safe-keeping for possible future identification of the writer?
     a)_____ b)_____ c)_____

4. Is your leisure-time reading of magazines generally (a) limited to one or two types or fields, or (b) spread over several types or fields?   a)_____ b)_____

5. If it rains to spoil your plans for an afternoon of golf or your favorite outdoor pastime (a) are you upset and grumpy most of the afternoon (b) do you find some other diversion, or (c) do you go ahead and play in the rain?   a)_____ b)_____ c)_____

6. If a pupil is late to your class because another teacher ran her class overtime, would you (a) report it to the principal (b) require the pupil to return to the other teacher for an excuse, or (c) overlook the incident unless it happens frequently?
     a)_____ b)_____ c)_____

7. Would you rather (a) prepare a speech, or (b) deliver it?
     a)_____ b)_____

8. If, as a superintendent, you were dismissing a teacher, would you (a) send her a letter notifying her of the fact (b) notify her in a private conference, or (c) announce it at board meeting?
     a)_____ b)_____ c)_____

9. Do you compromise often in your arguments?
     Yes_____ No_____

10. If a high school senior confided in you as a teacher or administrator that she was pregnant, would you (a) advise her to inform her parents immediately (b) recommend that she be expelled from school, or (c) recommend that she not be permitted to receive a diploma?   a)_____ b)_____ c)_____

11. Do you work effectively only with (*a*) people (*b*) things (*c*) ideas, or (*d*) each about equally well when the situation requires it? *a*)____ *b*)____ *c*)____ *d*)____

12. Have you of your own choosing rearranged the furniture in your classroom or office (*a*) more than or (*b*) fewer than two times during the past year? *a*)____ *b*)____

13. If a classmate copies from you during an exam and receives a better mark than you, would you (*a*) explain the incident to the instructor (*b*) discuss it with the classmate who copied, or (*c*) do nothing about it and try to forget the matter?

a)____ *b*)____ *c*)____

14. Would you rather (*a*) play social or mixing games at a party, or (*b*) chat with your acquaintances there? *a*)____ *b*)____

15. Are you usually more intrigued with the anticipation of reading (*a*) a scientific treatise (*b*) biography of a great person, or (*c*) a book on investments and banking? *a*)____ *b*)____ *c*)____

16. Would you be frightened to be a passenger on the first space trip to the moon? Yes____ No____

17. If you appeared in acceptable business dress at your club's dance which you have been anticipating, and discovered that all the other members were garbed in formal evening attire, would you (*a*) remain and enjoy yourself (*b*) quietly make your exit, or (*c*) stay in the background as an onlooker?

a)____ *b*)____ *c*)____

18. Do you enjoy (*a*) participating in group singing (*b*) taking a walk in the woods alone (*c*) attending a sporting event, or (*d*) each about equally well under some circumstances?

a)____ *b*)____ *c*)____ *d*)____

19. When you are caught in a slow-moving traffic snarl on the way to an important appointment, do you (*a*) neglect ordinary rules of driving courtesy (*b*) observe proper driving regulations and make the best of it, or (*c*) take risky chances that endanger lives? *a*)____ *b*)____ *c*)____

20. Assuming that you don't drink alcoholic beverages and your host at a party is obnoxiously insistent that you have one, would you (*a*) thank him and repeat that you don't drink (*b*) inform him indignantly that you don't drink, or (*c*) accept his offer but discreetly avoid drinking it? *a*)____ *b*)____ *c*)____

21. Generally, would you rather spend an evening (*a*) with friends, or (*b*) making or fixing some object at home?

a)_____ *b*)_____

22. Do you usually experience a sense of (*a*) pleasure or (*b*) displeasure in looking forward to the change in seasons?

a)_____ *b*)_____

23. Do you frequently try to find a different and untried road to a destination where you must go numerous times?

Yes_____ No_____

24. In a college class when you volunteered an obviously stupid answer to the professor's question, did you (*a*) laugh at yourself (*b*) want to crawl under the desk, or (*c*) refrain from volunteering again in that class?   *a*)_____ *b*)_____ *c*)_____

25. Do you find satisfactory relaxation, diversion, and enjoyment in (*a*) more than, or (*b*) fewer than five different forms of entertainment?   *a*)_____ *b*)_____

26. Do you find it fairly (*a*) easy, or (*b*) difficult to start conversations with strangers?   *a*)_____ *b*)_____

27. When voting in the organizations to which you belong do you more frequently find yourself voting (*a*) with, or (*b*) against the majority?   *a*)_____ *b*)_____

28. Assuming the same income if you were a clerk in a department store, would you rather sell (*a*) several items with frequent sales, or (*b*) a large item with fewer customers? *a*)_____ *b*)_____

29. Assuming that you had the appropriate training, would you enjoy more working in an industrial plant as (*a*) an accountant (*b*) personnel manager, or (*c*) manager of the shipping department?   *a*)_____ *b*)_____ *c*)_____

30. Do you like to gamble on the long shots?   Yes_____ No_____

31. In your lifetime, have you on (*a*) more than, or (*b*) fewer than three different occasions written to the editor of a newspaper or magazine to correct a printed error or to express your point of view?   *a*)_____ *b*)_____

32. In teaching the same class over a period of years, do you (*a*) primarily follow identical lesson plans, or (*b*) try different approaches and techniques.   *a*)_____ *b*)_____

33. After a particularly tiring day, if you find that the wife has rearranged the furniture, including displacing your favorite easy

chair from your choice location, would you (*a*) return the chair to its former location without comment (*b*) relax satisfactorily where the chair is now, or (*c*) praise her ideas but suggest that you preferred the former arrangement? *a*)_____ *b*)_____ *c*)_____

34. Should a group of "radical" ministers appear at a board meeting requesting that square dancing be eliminated from physical education classes for moral reasons, would you as superintendent (*a*) explain that the protest is ridiculous and that square dancing is wholesome recreation (*b*) agree to discontinue the square dancing, or (*c*) suggest that you might discuss the matter with a faculty committee? *a*)_____ *b*)_____ *c*)_____

35. Would you rather (*a*) act in a play, or (*b*) be the author of the play? *a*)_____ *b*)_____

36. In the organizations to which you belong have you (*a*) frequently, or (*b*) infrequently been elected an officer?
a)_____ *b*)_____

37. On your first trip to strange places are you inclined to (*a*) follow the guidebook or the advice of others, or (*b*) venture on your own? *a*)_____ *b*)_____

38. After a day which brings more reversals than approvals, do you (*a*) sleep as well as usual (*b*) roll and toss much of the night, or (*c*) take some action to induce sleep before retiring?
a)_____ *b*)_____ *c*)_____

39. Do you enjoy humorous stories (*a*) with a clean, clever punch line (*b*) the slightly off-color variety (*c*) about school children, or (*d*) each about equally well under appropriate circumstances? *a*)_____ *b*)_____ *c*)_____ *d*)_____

40. If you discover a page torn out of an especially enjoyable book which you're reading, do you (*a*) discontinue reading the book (*b*) go ahead and finish the story, or (*c*) do something else for awhile? *a*)_____ *b*)_____ *c*)_____

41. During the question-and-answer period following a lecture or discussion, do you (*a*) frequently, or (*b*) rarely ask questions?
a)_____ *b*)_____

42. In time of war would you rather (*a*) be drafted into military service, or (*b*) volunteer? *a*)_____ *b*)_____

43. If the operator should cut you off in the midst of an important long distance telephone conversation, are you most likely to

(*a*) scold her (*b*) notify her of her mistake and ask her to re-establish the connection, or (*c*) say nothing to her since everyone makes mistakes?   *a*)_____ *b*)_____ *c*)_____

44. Do you find it extremely difficult and embarrassing to admit your mistakes?   Yes_____ No_____

45. When you are the object of a practical joke concocted by acquaintances, do you (*a*) manage to prevent your annoyance from showing (*b*) quit associating with that crowd, or (*c*) caution them about the potential dangers of practical jokes?

a)_____ *b*)_____ *c*)_____

46. Are your free Saturdays generally spent (*a*) in a similar pattern, or (*b*) is there quite a difference in activities from one Saturday to the other?   *a*)_____ *b*)_____

47. When you encounter a road detour, do you usually (*a*) study the map before proceeding (*b*) follow the detour signs without delay, or (*c*) express your disgust with the highway department?

a)_____ *b*)_____ *c*)_____

48. If your hostess expresses disappointment that you didn't try her appetizer which you despise, would you (*a*) say that you never could stand the stuff (*b*) explain that you're too full, or (*c*) fabricate some excuse why you can't eat it?

a)_____ *b*)_____ *c*)_____

49. Would you rather (*a*) plan and design a new school building, or (*b*) work actively to promote the bond issue which makes the building possible?   *a*)_____ *b*)_____

50. If one of your capable students refuses to work after you have tried every motivating device at your command, would you (*a*) recommend that he repeat the course or grade (*b*) refer him to the pupil counseling personnel for study, or (*c*) promote him on the basis of his known ability?   *a*)_____ *b*)_____ *c*)_____

51. Does the anticipation of a holiday, your birthday, or party ofttimes get you "keyed up" to the point of hindering concentration on your work?   Yes_____ No_____

52. When friends and close acquaintances die, do you (*a*) attend the funeral or visit the funeral home as a matter of course (*b*) visit the funeral home and sign the register but not view the body, or (*c*) avoid the funeral and visitation altogether—just send a note or flowers?   *a*)_____ *b*)_____ *c*)_____

53. Do you enjoy wearing (*a*) a business suit (*b*) sportswear (*c*) formal evening clothes, or (*d*) each about equally well under appropriate circumstances?   *a*)_____ *b*)_____ *c*)_____ *d*)_____

54. Would you prefer a teaching assignment with (*a*) all classes in one subject field and/or grade level, or (*b*) a mixture?
a)_____ *b*)_____

55. If four board members are ready to vote on an issue but you, as superintendent, detect that the fifth is hesitating because he doesn't understand it, would you (*a*) recommend that the vote be taken now (*b*) explain the matter a third time even though it requires about twenty minutes to do it, or (*c*) suggest that you should have obtained more complete information and that the matter be tabled until you've had an opportunity to do so?
a)_____ *b*)_____ *c*)_____

56. Would you rather (*a*) serve as host or receptionist for a dance, or (*b*) serve on the decorating committee? *a*)_____ *b*)_____

57. In your political voting do you (*a*) usually vote your party ticket but occasionally vote for a candidate of the other party (*b*) always vote the straight party ticket, or (*c*) frequently vote for more candidates in the other party than in your own?
a)_____ *b*)_____ *c*)_____

58. Have you (*a*) often (*b*) occasionally, or (*c*) rarely been considered a "radical" thinker by your acquaintances?
a)_____ *b*)_____ *c*)_____

59. If you were the first to come upon a badly smashed car on the road, would you (*a*) stop to see if you can help the victims (*b*) slow down and then go to the nearest phone to call for help, or (*c*) pass by for fear of what you might find in the wreckage?
a)_____ *b*)_____ *c*)_____

60. Would you prefer (*a*) joining in a philosophical discussion (*b*) appearing on a panel discussion (*c*) reading a book (*d*) or would you enjoy each about equally well under appropriate circumstances?   *a*)_____ *b*)_____ *c*)_____ *d*)_____

61. If your friends drop in during your favorite television program, do you (*a*) invite them to enjoy the show with you knowing that they don't care for it (*b*) turn off the program to enjoy your callers, or (*c*) turn off the contraption with enough display of disgust so that they won't do it again? *a*)_____ *b*)_____ *c*)_____

62. Do you more often buy clothing (*a*) on impulse, or (*b*) after

studied judgment or deliberate planning?   *a*)_____ *b*)_____

63. Would you rather take a scenic trip (*a*) alone, or (*b*) with friends?   *a*)_____ *b*)_____

64. If a colleague asks you to sign a petition in favor of another colleague's bid for a professional office and you don't regard the candidate as suitable, would you (*a*) say so and refuse to sign (*b*) postpone signing with the explanation that you want to think it over, or (*c*) sign and regret it?   *a*) _____ *b*)_____ *c*)_____

65. If a fire should start in your classroom wastebasket while class is in session, which action would you take first? (*a*) Try to put out the fire. (*b*) Get the pupils out of the building. (*c*) Call the fire department.   *a*)_____ *b*)_____ *c*)_____

66. When you dine at a strange but reputable restaurant, do you usually (*a*) try new foods and dishes, or (*b*) order those which you know you'll enjoy?   *a*)_____ *b*)_____

67. If the principal calls an unscheduled assembly of students for an important matter, do you as a teacher (*a*) remind him that he should announce assemblies in advance (*b*) adjust your teaching plans accordingly with little personal reaction, or (*c*) experience a sense of frustration for having your schedule upset?
          a)_____ *b*)_____ *c*)_____

68. If you were being introduced along with other honored guests at a community banquet and the master of ceremonies mispronounced your name, would you (*a*) correct him before rising to accept the recognition (*b*) show your annoyance because he didn't know you, or (*c*) accept the introduction as if it had been correct?   *a*)_____ *b*)_____ *c*)_____

69. Would you enjoy more (*a*) being a lab assistant in research that leads to a significant discovery, or (*b*) teaching others the uses and implications of the discovery?   *a*)_____ *b*)_____

70. Are you generally (*a*) the first to try out a new idea or technique, or (*b*) do you prefer to wait for the results of others who have tried it?   *a*)_____ *b*)_____

ANSWERS AND QUALITIES RATED IN APTITUDE-INTEREST TEST
Directions: The correct answers for the purpose of this test appear below for each question. After the answer there are listed in Roman numerals (and in brackets) the qualities which are being measured by the question. In scoring your answers, ignore the

Roman numerals for the time being. Compare the answers below with your responses to the 70 questions, checking off (√) below each answer which does not agree with your answer.

1. Yes (I)
2. No (I)
3. *a*) (II, V, VII)
4. *b*) (III)
5. *b*) (IV)
6. *c*) (II, IV, V, VII)
7. *b*) (VI)
8. *b*) (II, V, VII)
9. Yes (I, V, VII)
10. *a*) (II, V, VII)
11. *d*) (III, IV)
12. *a*) (III)
13. *c*) (II, IV, V, VII)
14. *a*) (III, VI)
15. *b*) (VI, VII)
16. Yes (I)
17. *a*) (II, IV, VI`
18. *d*) (III, IV)
19. *b*) (II, IV)
20. *c*) (IV, V, VII)
21. *a*) (VI)
22. *a*) (III, IV)
23. Yes (I, III)
24. *a*) (II)
25. *a*) (III, IV)
26. *a*) (VI)
27. *a*) (I)
28. *a*) (III, VI)
29. *b*) (VI, VII)
30. No (I)
31. *b*) (II, V)
32. *b*) (I, III)
33. *b*) (II, III, IV, V, VII)
34. *c*) (V, VII)
35. *a*) (VI)

36. *a*) (VI)
37. *b*) (I, III)
38. *a*) (II)
39. *d*) (III, IV)
40. *b*) (II, IV)
41. *a*) (I, VI)
42. *b*) (I, VI)
43. *b*) (II, IV, V, VII)
44. No (I, II)
45. *a*) (II, IV, V, VI, VII)
46. *b*) (III)
47. *b*) (II, IV)
48. *c*) (V, VII)
49. *b*) (VI)
50. *b*) (V, VII)
51. No (II)
52. *a*) (II, V, VII)
53. *d*) (III)
54. *b*) (III)
55. *c*) (V, VII)
56. *a*) (VI)
57. *a*) (I)
58. *c*) (I)
59. *a*) (II, IV)
60. *d*) (III)
61. *b*) (IV, V, VI, VII)
62. *b*) (I)
63. *b*) (VI)
64. *b*) (V, VII)
65. *a*) (II, IV)
66. *a*) (I, III)
67. *b*) (II, IV, V, VII)
68. *c*) (II, IV, V, VII)
69. *b*) (VI)
70. *b*) (I)

SCALED RESULTS OF APTITUDE-INTEREST TEST

Directions: For each question in the Aptitude-Interest Test answered correctly, place a check mark on the appropriate scale below of Figure IV that corresponds to the Roman numeral, or numerals, appearing in brackets beside the answer on page 190. For example, if you answered correctly Question 1, place a check mark ($\sqrt{}$) to the right of Scale I below. If you answered correctly Question 2, place a check mark in the next block to the right. Some questions measure more than one quality, and therefore will have more than one Roman numeral beside the answer. Place a check mark on each scale as indicated if you answered that question correctly. Make no check marks below if you answered the question incorrectly. You will advance on the scale according to correct answers only. Your total score for each of the seven qualities being measured will be the farthest block to the right checked in each scale.

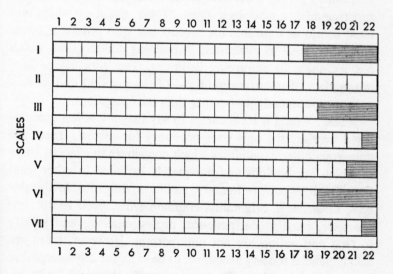

Figure IV. Scale for measuring results of test

Legend of Qualities Measured
Scale I—Progressive conservatism
Scale II—Stoicism
Scale III—Divergent interests
Scale IV—Adaptability
Scale V—Diplomacy
Scale VI—Gregarious personality
Scale VII—Understanding of human nature

The Seven Most Important Personal Qualities for Successful Superintendency

Surely the reader will have observed throughout this volume a meticulous avoidance of dogmatic assertions as to any qualities or work habits that will guarantee success in administering a school system. There still exists too much instability in the position to permit a precise job analysis. Cases are known of superintendents who lack most of the qualities which are cited herein as desirable for success but who possess a single capability, such as expertness in building construction, which has led them to rewarding positions. The conclusions here are predicated upon generalities—of the position and of successful superintendents—rather than the exceptions.

Neither would it be accurate to say that the seven qualities listed here are the only ones necessary for success. There are numerous other capabilities which contribute to success, some of which are obvious and adequately included in other treatises. Qualities such as honesty, ambition, diligence, forthrightness, shrewdness, originality, common sense, good health, appearance, intelligence, patience, professionalism, and loyalty to God and nation are not unimportant. However, these are also beneficial for any executive; to be sure, for any acceptable occupation in society. They are virtually the same traits incorporated in the Boy Scout oath.

This test seeks to focus attention on those qualities that are essential for the unique occupation of public school superintendency. It will also be noticed that most are characteristics which are, for some unknown reason, overlooked in the journalistic treatments of the superintendency, or at best, are only hinted at through implication.

The seven most desirable personal qualities for successful school administration in the opinion of the author are progressive conservatism, stoicism, divergent interests, adaptability, diplomacy, gregarious personality, and understanding of human nature. The order as listed does not reflect any priority of importance.

PROGRESSIVE CONSERVATISM

In a sense this is a way of saying nothing, which might be helpful if some superintendents would work at it. What the term is meant to imply is that the extremes on any issue are to be avoided by a successful superintendent. It is perhaps good advice for anyone. A good share, if not most, of life's frictions are caused by people who see either black or white, and are color-blind to grays. J. H. Rhoades advised, "Be wary of extremes; the green and the overripe fruit cause the worst pain."

Of course this doesn't mean that a superintendent should not square his shoulders and stand firm when the occasion demands it. Interpreted literally, it would mean he could never make a decision. Obviously, no administrator can pursue this policy. At the other extreme, he cannot adopt the army maxim, "When you don't know what to do, do something." Again, there is a safer inbetween. There are superintendents who represent both extremes; those who know there is only one way of doing anything, and the ones who can never offer a clear-cut decision. None of these are successful. The would-be successful superintendent should have marked eleven or more correct answers on Scale I.

The modern superintendent does not fear the unknown, but respects it. He is sufficiently venturesome to experiment with new ideas and knows when it is safe to venture. At the same time he remembers that it is an experiment and is willing to back up if the facts indicate its advisability. He does not hesitate to admit his mistakes.

While the modern superintendent is progressive enough to explore uncharted areas, he is also sufficiently conservative to prevent leaping for every new fangle that appears in the profession. Experimenting with the unknown is meritorious if no one else is willing to do it, but there is nothing fusty about waiting for the results of another's experiment if it is already under way. Excessive starting and backing can be just as frustrating to a staff and community as no starting at all.

A progressive conservative does not always stay in the middle of the road. As comfortable as that location might be, he is not afraid to try another route. He is neither the first to follow nor the last to lead. In his philosophy and actions, he is a cautious daredevil.

STOICISM

Perhaps a better term would be thick-skinned. If an aspirant for the superintendency position did not score at least seventeen answers in this section of the test it is recommended that he talk with more practicing superintendents to assure himself that he can roll with the punches. If he checked fewer than ten correct answers, he should definitely remain in teaching. There should be no mistaking on this point—superintendency is a rough and tumble game, no pastime for the sensitive.

Possessing a Spartan nature is desirable for any executive position. Business administrators have, for the most part, mastered the quality or else they couldn't hang on in the no-holds-barred competition of factory, mine, sales office, or retail store. It is perhaps the most difficult attitude for the would-be superintendent to develop because most people who enter the teaching profession, and those who are generally the most successful teachers, are highly sensitive individuals. As such, it is one of the least expected characteristics demanded of the superintendent. Lacking the quality is undoubtedly the principal reason why many superintendents become unhappy in the work and either fail or leave for more comfortable occupations.

The ability to withstand criticism and attack is even more necessary for the superintendency than for many business occupations. A public figure invites abuse when he accepts office. The American attitude toward public office holders is characterized by irony. A citizen will fervently campaign for his choice candidate, but kick him in the pants at the slightest provocation. He invites the public figure to occupy the seat of honor at a ceremony one day but accuses him of treacherous deceit the next. He entrusts him with fabulous sums of money and almost expects him to misuse it.

It is difficult for a professional educator to understand how a layman can associate the administration of a public school with other public administrations, but somehow the citizen manages it. Historically, it is a tribute to the character of superintendents that the association obtains no more than it does. Nevertheless, in the minds of many, a school superintendent is just another public office holder and is entitled to no more immunity from attack than any other. The superintendent has to be able to take it.

The superintendent is also fair game for attack from within. Many teachers, particularly labor unionists in the profession, assume automatically that a superintendent takes on qualities foreign to education the moment he is appointed. It is imagined that he immediately loses all recollections of teacher viewpoints and problems. He becomes administration, not education; management as opposed to labor. Therefore, he is the symbol, or whipping boy, for all that ails teachers. The fact that he is the boss, makes more money, enjoys more community stature, and constitutes the fleshpot of professional advancement in the community stirs human resentments. Whether he earns it or not, he can expect considerable criticism from his subordinates.

If a superintendent expects to sleep at night and maintain necessary standards of physical well-being, he must pull about him a rhinoceros skin of impassioned emotion to withstand the verbal barbs, must learn to separate the chaff of fribble from matters of consequence that deserve attention and energy, and frequently must operate apart from the normal human behavior. It is helpful if the superintendent can acquire a philosophical attitude of looking through one-way vision glass at the antics of men and women trying desperately to satisfy their basic drives of life.

DIVERGENT INTERESTS

The questions which sought to measure this quality were so designed that one could scarcely avoid achieving at least twelve correct answers on Scale III. The purpose, of course, is to ascertain if one really enjoys variety. It is highly unlikely that a person narrow in interests, activities, or thinking will be either happy or successful in school administration.

Any reader who has come this far in the book certainly grasps the idea that a superintendent's dominion is extensive. Superintendents may become disgusted, frustrated, or fed up, but never bored. It offers too many challenges and too much multifariousness for the administrator to become static. It is vitally important, therefore, for a superintendent to enjoy variety.

It is almost as equally important that his non-professional interests are broad, not only because of his diverse responsibilities in the community but also because of the pressing need to relax and escape. A school administrator or teacher who spends all day with educational concerns and then of his own volition reads professional journals, or attends educational meetings every night becomes entirely too prosaic for the well-rounded job he is expected to do. Anyone so narrowly dedicated inevitably sacrifices something that contributes to the success of his job, or his life.

ADAPTABILITY

While the superintendent needs to adjust easily to the environments of different communities, the concern here is with his ability to adapt to rapidly changing situations and environments throughout the day. As indicated in Chapter II, his scope of activity is nearly boundless. Any one of these problems could be presented at any moment of the day, and he must have the talent for switching his chain of thought without becoming frantic.

These incidents actually occurred to the author within a five-minute span on a blustery fall day. While discussing a boy's behavior problem with the parents, one phone call from a principal informed him that a child had been hit by a car enroute to school; the private phone call from his wife, which rang before hanging up the other receiver, notified him what to bring home for dinner; the business manager interrupted to acquaint the superintendent with the fact that the furnace was down in one building and it would be necessary to send the children home; the secretary brought in a document for signature that had to catch the next mail delivery; the coach called for permission to cancel a football game; and a board member telephoned to advise that he wouldn't be present at the next meeting.

Now it could be claimed that an efficient administrator would have office routine so organized and duties adequately delegated as to avoid such interruptions. This can and should be done to a degree, but as indicated earlier, the public school superintendent cannot regulate his daily schedule as another executive might do. He either handles the situations as they arise or stacks up a line of smouldering problems and people outside his office door. The superintendent must stand ready to shift mental gears rapidly without stripping his emotional mechanism.

He must also be able to adapt himself to the different publics he encounters in the community. While he needn't, and can't be a dozen Jekyls and a dozen Hydes, the expectations of varying groups are not identical. There are certain common traits of behavior which the superintendent should exemplify to all people, but the service club may expect joviality while the WCTU expects somber morality. The PTA expects educational leadership while the student body looks to him for regulation. The library board seeks his intellectual capacity, while the athletic booster club tests his sporting blood. Teachers may want his administrative talent, while the poker club is interested in his conviviality. The chamber of commerce may sample his sense of economy, while the labor union is interested in his welfare attitudes. There need be no conflict with sincerity in adjusting to this variety of expectations, but for the daily shifting scenes, some superintendents cannot find enough costumes to please the audience. It would be hoped that the student checked correctly at least fifteen answers on Scale IV.

DIPLOMACY

The commander of an autocratic organization, or the business tycoon who owns 51 per cent of the stock, can accomplish his mission without any diplomacy. A superintendent of schools enjoys no such advantage. In fact, he is in the peculiar command position of having to get things done by people who can also fire him. On the one hand he is expected to direct their actions—citizens, board members, teachers, and students—and on the other hand he is their hired hand. Any segment of his command can be the force which leads to his being relieved of command. This charge calls for as much diplomacy as any state ambassadorship with portfolio.

A candidate who failed to mark correctly more than twelve answers on Scale V might well discuss with his wife the practicability of considering another profession for a livelihood, since tact and diplomacy are essential for a successful teacher as well as for an administrator.

An absolutist may have missed a few of the test questions on the grounds that the correct answer would involve stretching the truth under certain circumstances. It resurrects the age-old ethical debate as to whether or not a "white lie" is ever justified. There is no desire on the part of the author to encourage compromising of truth if it offends one's code of honor. The advice is submitted, however, that brutal frankness can be as damaging as polite untruth designed to avoid personal hurt.

There has been created over the years a variety of caustic definitions of a diplomat, but it is intended herein to mean only knowing "What to do when." The oft-mentioned significance of timing one's moves is really part of administrative diplomacy. Personality, too, is a part of diplomacy.

The diplomatic superintendent can be likened accurately unto an experienced puppeteer, who is in the background pulling the appropriate string for movement forward, then the halt string, the string of reverse, sidestep, surreptitious prodding, full steam ahead, lullaby, kick, playing possum, and bow. The puppeteer has the advantage, though. He has only two handfuls of strings to manage.

GREGARIOUS PERSONALITY

It is a flimsy but remarkable truism that a man can perform at sub-par level in practically any undertaking and he'll get along if people like him. It is decidedly true for the school superintendent as suggested previously. He can demonstrate many weaknesses, but he'll seldom lose his job, might even advance, if he is well liked by the community and staff. Some men with mediocre talents have parlayed a slap on the back, a packet of jokes, and a ready smile into the top positions of the country. Conversely, some highly skilled administrators have struggled to keep their contracts alive because of bankrupt personalities.

There have been numerous investigations to determine the relationship of popularity or likeableness to leadership. In all of the studies known to the author, popularity scored a favorable correlation with leadership, in one instance higher than any other trait except originality.[1]

A prospective superintendent who scored fewer than twelve correct answers on Scale VI had better start now, if it's not later than he thinks, to seek competent advice on how to develop a pleasant demeanor.

It is scarcely enough to possess a pleasing personality. One can have the trigger cocked for a smile when approached but too shy to seek out his quarry. A superintendent should be gregarious with his personality.

UNDERSTANDING OF HUMAN NATURE

The superintendent's need for this quality is obviously no monopoly. It's necessary for success in every trade, to include thievery. So much has already been said about it in this book that it would need no elaboration here if it weren't basic to all the goals and techniques mentioned herein, and if it weren't for the extent of its neglect in the profession. A superintendency candidate should have scored at least fifteen correct answers on Scale VII.

A Ford Motor Company vice-president, in his convocation address before the students and faculty of Occidental College, summarized the urgency of this quality as follows:

The technical problems we can lick—the really tough problems are people. To work with people well, you will have to understand them—how they act and react and, insofar as possible, why they react as they do. You will have to size them up—their demonstrated and especially their potential abilities.[2]

---

[1] Ralph M. Stogdill, "Personal Factors Associated with Leadership: A Survey of the Literature," *Journal of Psychology* (1948) Vol. 25, pp. 35-71.
[2] Theodore O. Yntema, "A Liberal Education," an address; The Ford Motor Company, Dearborn, Mich., May 10, 1957.

Consider the importance to the superintendent of knowing what makes people tick, and being able to anticipate their reactions, in achieving his objectives with teachers, board members, students, staff, and laymen; for timing his moves, for public relations, for getting a job, and for public speaking.

At initial glance there may appear to be a conflict between this requirement for a successful superintendent and the plea for stoicism. How can one be understanding of human behavior and still be dispassionate? The conflict is more apparent than real. A stoic demeanor protects the superintendent from the lack of human understanding among others, but he will still need to understand human nature in order to gain his ends. The adroit poker player exemplifies the difference. From behind the artificial boundaries of a few cards, he studies the reactions of his counterparts to facilitate his decisions, but he does not permit their behavior to disturb his own equanimity.

So You Flunked the Test

It is hoped you are discouraged about entering the superintendency profession if you did not perform well on this test. If your self-analyses were completed candidly, and if your responses disagreed immoderately with the recommended answers, it is strongly suggested that you give further serious consideration to your desires for a life in superintendency. Your predictive capacity for enjoyment of it and success in it are not eminent.

However, there are consolation prizes. In the first place, it should be re-emphasized that no test has complete reliability. Moreover, no present obstacles or possible future ones can often defeat a man in reaching his goals if his drive is strong enough. If that desire is superlative, he will undoubtedly do something about correcting the shortcomings revealed by the test. And finally, one cannot overlook fortuity in evaluating any career. The breaks of the game play a prominent role in achieving a goal. As has been indicated again and again, there is no pattern of preparation or activity that will *guarantee* success or failure in the superintendency.

chapter eleven

Get Ready! Get Set!

The second step in the process of developing capable administrators is the completion of their professional preparation. Assuming that the student demonstrates adequate aptitude and interest for the work, or even that he has dogged determination to become a superintendent despite unfavorable performance on the test, he is ready to undertake his formal training. What should it be? This chapter suggests a program geared specifically to answering that question.

An analysis of the various administrative preparatory programs in existence reveals the peculiar concepts held by university personnel regarding the nature of the superintendency occupation. Some programs show that the prevailing interpretations of the superintendent's job on those campuses are that he is primarily an educator, and hence his preparatory experiences are loaded with philosophy, curricular content, teaching methods, and general education. In fact, the Ph.D. program conceives the job as fundamentally that of a culturist or humanitarian.

Other programs indicate the superintendent is basically a form-filler and a thing-doer. Presumably, he minds the store and is an expert financier, businessman, and construction contractor.

Still others are beginning to suggest that the superintendent is the organization man, a sort of executive or manager of a trusteeship.

To say that any of these approaches is wrong is to introduce further conceptualization. It is a fact, however, that the modern superintendent is all of these—and more. The author's concept sees the superintendent first and foremost as one who performs his mission by working for, with, and through people. A preparatory program, therefore, should give major emphasis to exercises that sharpen his operative skill in human relations.

In addition, he needs most of the training demanded in other concepts of the superintendency. It could appear that it is being advocated that he needs to know everything about everything. As helpful as this achievement might be, it is obviously impractical. It becomes equally obvious, however, that the trainee cannot afford to waste time in traditional mental gymnastics which have little relation to preparing him for the complex assignment he is expected to fulfill as a school superintendent. Professors of educational administration are challenged to build a training program tailored specifically for his needs.

Basic Principles Underlying the Graduate Program in Educational Administration

Several hypotheses are accepted as valid in designing the graduate program for training school administrators. Some of these are a repetition of propositions cited earlier herein but are listed again for the purpose at hand. Others have not been referred to previously in this volume but constitute the necessary foundation for structuring the program.

In the first place, *professional preparation for the work of superintendency is an essential ingredient for success*. There appears to be sufficient evidence to justify the conclusion that boards of education hold this qualification in high regard today when seeking candidates for vacancies. Despite the exceptions of those individuals who have been converted into capable administrators via the unnecessarily lengthy and difficult way of learning through trial and error on the job, formal professional instruction is desired by boards of their candidates. It may be apparent, but for the benefit of the skeptical, it is also accepted as a truth that "book larnin" can produce a professionally trained administrator.

School administration is a distinctive occupation requiring technical skills and specialized knowledge. It is akin to other types of executive endeavor and to other forms of educational activity, but not identical with any other work.

No training program can be fashioned that will prepare a superintendent for every situation and problem that he will encounter. The variation in the work and the scope of a superintendent's jurisdiction have been stressed throughout this book. Moreover, neither society, education, nor life itself is unchanging. The preparatory program, therefore, should be in tune with the common nature and the repetitive activities of the superintendency.

Failures in superintendency are attributed more to inability to work with people than to any other debility. It will be recalled that this fact constituted the premise for this book. A proper training program should aim to reduce failures.

It is expected that the superintendent will serve as the educational technical advisor to the board of education, the community, and the staff. As such he must be the best informed person in the community on all phases of education in general and on school administration specifically.

The professional training program for the school top executive should be built around the actual functions of most superintendents more than what a philosophy suggests they ought to be. Use of the phrase "more than" should be noted. This assumption does not deny the need for stimulating superintendents' thoughts along philosophical and idealistic avenues. However, the primary effort of the training program should be leveled toward helping a superintendent to do well those things which he is going to have to do in day-by-day operations. Although most human action is predicated upon some philosophy, either recognized or dormant, it seems conclusive that educational activity is influenced more by the interplay of local persons and events than by philosophical tenets.

A superintendent should possess more than speaking acquaintanceship with all subject matter offered by elementary and secondary schools. Since nearly all school administrators have advanced from teaching positions, each is a specialist in one, two, or three subjects in which he was prepared as an undergraduate and on which he has become an authority to some degree. It is only natural that as chief executive he will favor those departments to the neglect of others. This is, of course, unfair to both the pupils and the teachers. Therefore, some provision must be allowed for his developing familiarity with the content, values, objectives, and teaching methods of all curricular areas from kindergarten through high school, special education, extracurricular activities, and the lesser known services of a modern educational program.

Because of the continuing increase in population and birth rate anticipated for the next quarter century at least, *superintendents will be spending considerable time in constructing school buildings.* More than at any time in the history of public education, except during the past decade, superintendents will have to know more about the dozens of entailments in the planning and erecting of school buildings. A concomitant duty, of course, will be the raising of funds to enable the buildings.

The housekeeping chores in school administration will continue to be a necessary part of the superintendent's work— law, finance, plant maintenance, business management, personnel, supervision, and record keeping.

General knowledge is also an important element in the modern superintendent's success. In order to feel secure with all strata of a community's population, and in order to render intelligent decisions compatible with cultural patterns of the past and present, a superintendent must be grounded in what is commonly labeled "general education."

Not all persons are suited for administrative work, regardless of training. Consequently, universities have an obligation to reduce wasted effort and money of individuals as well as of their own resources and facilities.

Expertness in research and foreign languages is a negligible factor in contributing to the success of school administrators. Superintendents have less need for mastery of these disciplines than they have for familiarity with the various subject matters offered in the typical school. And yet the Ph.D. candidate in school administration who is pursuing the standard agenda spends at least one-third of his total required time in battling the two hurdles of dissertation and foreign languages. Probably the outstanding proposal of the thirty-five recently recommended by the A.A.S.A.'s Committee for the Advancement of School Administration is this one: "The school administrator is a practitioner, not a researcher, and the research required of him in professional training will recognize this distinction."[1] This conclusion coincides partially with the practice in some graduate training institutions of awarding the Doctor of Education degree instead of the Doctor of Philosophy degree.

And finally, *it is assumed that the well-established principle of "learning by doing" is as valid for the training of school superintendents as it is for teaching pupils.* Therefore, a good school administrator's training program makes some provision for practical application of the knowledge being learned before shoving him out of his training nest.

Criteria for Admitting Students to Graduate Training in Administration

Much of the concern about improving the quality of educational administration could be alleviated if more attention were given to the quality of person admitted to professional training. Admittedly, universities cannot be held responsible for the

[1] *Something to Steer By,* No. 17, Committee for Advancement of School Administrators, A.A.S.A., January 1958.

calibre of superintendent which boards of education select "in the field," but they can exert effective influence on the quality of administrator who parades under the banner of a professionally trained superintendent.

It seems logical that graduate colleges should require some successful classroom teaching experience before permitting a candidate to apply for admission. A prerequisite of at least two to five years of teaching is not unreasonable for a person to discover whether he is interested in administration and for his supervisors to detect signs of administrative potential. Requiring letters of recommendation from a candidate's superintendent is of value in learning whether a teacher demonstrates qualities that make for executive leadership. As will be elaborated upon later, this experience requirement has disadvantages from a financial point of view, but it is still advisable.

An appropriate battery of entrance tests is the best device yet developed for determining fitness for training. An aptitude and interest test, such as offered in the preceding chapter, or some comparable instrument, should be required of the candidate. In addition, some adequate evaluation of one's general knowledge is desirable. Certainly a personality adjustment test is needed. The specification of a minimum of 110 IQ is reasonable. It should also be required that the applicant establish competency in oral and written English.

CONTINUAL EVALUATION NEEDED DURING TRAINING PERIOD

With a good screening procedure, and as a candidate demonstrates adequate academic progress, it is still possible that the student will reveal weaknesses that can be detected best in the camaraderie of professor and student. It is recommended, therefore, that an advisory committee of at least three representative faculty members should counsel with the trainee periodically during the preparatory program.

If the committee becomes convinced of a student's inadequacies for the superintendency, it should have the courage and authority to remove him from the program.

General Areas of Preparation

The proposed program for the complete professional preparation of school superintendents may be classified into six areas of concentration. The three-year program makes no effort to distinguish between a Master's degree and a Doctor's degree under the assumption that a complete training can have no compromise. The only omissions from the prescribed program which might be contemplated are in the areas of general education where the student may have completed a major study in a particular subject as an undergraduate or demonstrates adequate competency therein.

The six areas, and the order in which they should be pursued, are:

General education
Professional education
Human relations and personality development
School administration
Executive management
Internship

Recommended areas for specific study, and around which courses can be built within the above general framework, are cited in Table V, page 210.

NO DISSERTATION OR FOREIGN LANGUAGE REQUIRED

Congruously with one of the earlier cited hypotheses, the proposed program for the Doctor's degree in school superintendency requires no dissertation or mastery of foreign languages. This issue, long discussed by university faculties, continues as a very live debate. Apparently, the defenders of the scholarly reputation of a Doctor's degree remain in the driver's seat, for the only concession granted thus far by some universities is the relaxing of the foreign language requirement and awarding a Doctor of Education degree. There are a few movements toward awarding a certificate for those who have completed the course work only.

Perhaps the mistake was made many moons ago during the early efforts to professionalize the school administrator. Perhaps this type of practitioner should not have been drawn into the aura of a doctorate. Perhaps the future solution of the dilemma lies in the correction of a past mistake—by developing a new label for a professionally trained practitioner. And yet, a person who completes a graduate preparatory program comparable to that suggested herein is entitled to an "initial" status equivalent to that enjoyed by graduates of other doctoral training programs.

TABLE V

RECOMMENDED AREA OF CONCENTRATION FOR DOCTOR'S DEGREE IN SCHOOL ADMINISTRATION

General Education
    Philosophy (General)
    Anthropology
    Sociology
    Economics
    Political Science
Professional Education
    History of Education
    Philosophy of Education
    Elementary Education (curriculum content, goals, methods in all study areas kindergarten through sixth grade)
    Secondary Education (curriculum content, goals, methods in all study areas seventh through twelfth grades)
    Special Education (orientation to entire field, to include pupil personnel services)
    Research Techniques

Human Relations and Personality Development
  Psychology (applied, motivational, self-analysis, behavior)
  Public Relations
  Public Speaking
  Group Processes
  Leadership Theory and Techniques
  Community Structure and Interaction
School Administration
  Introduction to Field of School Administration
  School Law
  Public School Finance
  School Business Management
  School Building Planning and Construction (including some
    basic principles of architecture and constructional engineer-
    ing).
  School Maintenance (to include buildings, mechanical installa-
    tions, equipment, and sites).
Executive Management
  Supervision of Learning and Teaching
  Personnel Management (including labor relations, welfare
    benefits).
  Administrative Organization (including office management, re-
    port writing, decision-making processes).
  Superintendent-board Relations
Administrative Internship
  (At least one-half year)

No quarrel can be found with the requirement for foreign
languages and dissertation research in either the liberal arts
specialties or in those vocational fields in which the graduate
will have need for those disciplines. Neither is the assumption
valid that the omission of these exercises for professionally
trained school administrators reflects upon the scholarly ca-
pacities of such trainees. Furthermore, it should not be concluded that the need for research in school administration is
lacking. Quite to the contrary. A difficulty is encountered,
however, when a topic for research is sought that is both
worthwhile and reasonable to expect of a student. The worth-

while problems are of such magnitude that a candidate could not complete the study in the time normally allotted for the activity. The team research approach as used by some universities is meritorious in this respect but can seldom be utilized since a university rarely has that many candidates ready for the dissertation step at one time. Even if there were, the amount of time which a student devotes to research stirs again the pestiferous question, "Does the training value of such research justify the effort?"

Consequently, the topics too frequently approved for doctoral dissertations amount to shallow compromises. It would appear that the criteria for approval adopted by some advisers would run something like this: "No one has yet brought these particular facts together under one binding; I believe it ought to take about a year to assemble the data and another six months to write it and rewrite it the standard number of times; and besides, I might be able to use the information sometime." For support of this contention one needs only to peruse the topics of doctoral dissertations, or consider the number of such projects that remain unpublished. And certainly education colleges have no monopoly on the use of these criteria.

The point of view being advocated here does not deny that a school administrator needs some knowledge of research techniques. He will have occasion to conduct, or supervise the conduct of, action research projects to improve the learning program in his school. While the nature of this research will more often be in the form of surveys, still a superintendent ought to be able to employ scientific investigational procedures. Furthermore, he should know enough about the techniques normally employed by researchers in order to evaluate the worthwhile studies that do appear in education. However, it is difficult to accept the notion that professional administrators need to undergo a year or more of personal research in order to understand the techniques of the game. If there ought to be a high correlation between a graduate training program and the nature of the trainee's vocation, and if the foreign language and dissertation requirements occupy one-third of the training program time, it is being said in effect that the practicing administrator will spend a third of his working time likewise!

The prevailing requirements pertaining to foreign languages and dissertation are reminiscent of the days when educational philosophy mandated Latin as a basis for understanding English, or for the doctor in order to write those mysterious messages on prescription slips. Most engineering colleges long ago eased their insistence upon students studying German before they pursued a formal training program for becoming engineers. Any correlation between competency in foreign languages and success in school administration is purely coincidental and is not intended to reflect upon the ability of an expert in either.

There are known cases of Ph.D. school administrators whose performance is of sub-par rating but who happened to be adept at digesting a foreign language. By the same token, there are some able executives roaming the nation's schools who could have brought further advancement, prestige, and improvement to themselves as well as to their school systems through acquiring a doctoral degree if they just hadn't flunked the foreign language examinations, or if they hadn't been at bat for the test when that particular faculty was in the negative cycle for granting Ph.D. degrees.

Admittedly, this plea for a more realistic attitude toward the foreign language requirement for school administrative doctorates is being reopened at an unpopular time. National tension of the moment centering about material achievements of certain other nationalities has aroused public concern over our educational programs for science, mathematics, and foreign languages. The inevitable comparisons of American educational systems with foreign programs, which is much like comparing a formal dinner with smorgasbord, has stimulated some school systems into adding another course in science, or moving the starting date for the study of foreign language

down another grade or two. When this current excitement has
given way to some other anxiety, educators must face again
this question, "How does the discipline of a study of foreign
language contribute any more to the quality of school administrators, or other practitioners who ought to complete a doctoral program to satisfy demands for a professionally trained
person, any more than a dozen other disciplines one might suggest, and which might be of more value to the student?" Some
scholars even find less mental challenge in the mastery of
another language than in understanding the workings of a
boiler.

SUPERINTENDENCY INTERNSHIP PREFERABLE

An apt comparison can be made between the purposes of
the graduate programs for school administration and the medical profession. Both types of doctors spend approximately an
equal length of time in preparation for their respective specialties. Medicine is a knowledge-plus-performance process. So is
schoolteaching. If rehearsing under real situations is good for
training doctors and teachers, it must be good for superintendents.

The preparatory program outline herein provides for one-
half year of practice administration. That should be considered
a minimum. The total training program could be flexible
enough to allow for more if it is possible to arrange. If the Admissions Committee should allow credit for certain courses
that the student might have completed adequately as an undergraduate, it is conceivable that he could spend a full year in-
terning.

The intern program should be structured to permit practice
under approved, capable administrators and should offer the
internee a variety of experiences. The plan should also be sufficiently elastic to allow experiences in which the candidate has
not previously participated. In addition to working directly
with superintendents, the program might include apprentice-

ship relations with the business manager and finance officer of a city school system, principals, the various supervisors and directors of a city system who perform specialty roles, and with community groups.

Some of the abortive efforts which have already been undertaken in this direction call for the candidate to be paid by the local board of education. This approach is likely to be fated for resistance from school boards, and perhaps staff personnel. The service which the intern will render to the local school system is going to be slight since he cannot be entrusted with authority for the short time he will be affiliated with the school. Moreover, most boards are confronted with a legal obstacle when they reimburse a quasi-employee under this practice, even if the idea is acceptable to local taxpayers and to teachers. Student teachers are not paid for their services; in fact, it frequently operates in reverse. The superintendency internship should be regarded as just another requirement of graduate work.

Financing the Graduate Program

There is one formidable block to the proposed graduate program for school administrators, and to all others—the matter of cost to the student. While the annual cost for the three years is no more severe than that for an undergraduate program, it comes at a period in life when the student can ill afford to undertake it.

This program recommends that a candidate for the Doctor's degree in school administration should have at least two to five years of classroom experience before commencing his graduate work. Quite often the candidates will have completed more years of teaching experience before making the plunge. But let us follow through the early life of a prospective administrator seeking professional preparation.

Usually a man is about twenty-two years of age upon completion of his Bachelor's degree. If he gives two years of service to the Armed Forces, he is twenty-four. By the time he has two to five years of teaching experience under his belt, he is twenty-six or twenty-nine. He ought to complete his doctoral program by the time he is thirty-five, no later than forty, if it is going to profit him as a tool for advancement.

Most men marry and have their families under way by the time they are thirty years of age. They have also made financial commitments toward furnishing a house and probably buying one. They are still low on the salary schedule, probably steeped in debt, undoubtedly have heavy expenses, and certainly have been unable to build up a reserve to invest in three years of graduate work without some form of income.

This is the precise age, between twenty-five and thirty-five, that a young man should be working on his doctorate. It is the same period in his life during which he can least afford it. This impasse is accountable for a substantial share of the lack of professionally trained superintendents throughout the land.

In order to do more than talk about improving the quality of superintendents, some thought must be given to solving the expense problem. An obvious answer, of course, is scholarships for administrative trainees. Some steps have already been taken in this direction, but they are so rare as to be negligible.

Many universities are offering working fellowships and graduate assistantship opportunities, all of which help but generally retard the process of getting the superintendent trained and back to earning a living for his growing family.

Universities can take a giant step toward solving the dilemma, as some of them already have, by discarding the requirement that a candidate for a Doctor's degree must spend a lengthy continuous period on campus and by permitting him to complete more work in summer sessions and piecemeal during the year. The cultural heritage which one is supposed to acquire by basking in the environment of a college campus is of controvertible value, especially for one who has already enjoyed that privilege for at least four years. The author is unfamiliar with any research that establishes the number of years it requires to soak up campus air, but an unscientific guess would be that it is something less than four years.

Still another possibility, but one which runs contrary to the recommendation herein, is to permit a student to push on to his Doctor's degree without the benefit of teaching experience. The disadvantages, though apparent, may be exaggerated. Doctoral work in other colleges generally follows this pattern. If it constitutes a means of assuring more professionally trained superintendents, however, it is certainly worth considering.

Graduate Training for Advanced Graduates

The discussion thus far has been directed toward those students who are commencing a graduate program in school administration from the Bachelor's degree level. This omits the second great source of future top school administrators, many of whom have already completed a Master's degree in school administration, or portions thereof. This category includes many of the men who are anxious to advance to better positions but have not yet discovered the key.

Professional training will not guarantee superintendency success for all of these administrators any more surely than one can develop race horses out of all plow horses, but a carefully planned program designed to shore up the weaknesses holds promise. The first step would be to administer to these candidates the battery of tests in order to uncover the weaknesses. The Admissions Committee should, again, exercise sufficient courage to refuse admittance to such applicants whose test results indicate little hope of their profiting from the graduate work. The training program should be flexible enough to permit planning a pattern of courses according to the needs of the person.

Timing Your Career

It is not a new idea, but for the administrator who wants to advance, he should plan his career by a timetable.

First, he ought to settle on his top goal, that position which he would like to be holding for the last fifteen or twenty years of his active working life. He should be there by the time he is forty-five, at least not later than fifty. Working back from this position by five-year intervals to where he now stands will provide a systematic plan of advancement. If he fails to schedule the intervening goals, he is apt to drift—perhaps a more comfortable way to pass one's lifetime but unrewarding insofar as attainment of high goals is concerned.

In deciding upon the steps of positions, it is not advisable to specify a definite school system. Too many accidents can happen for that. Limiting one's goal to a specific school could cause unwarranted frustration as a result of the disorganized pattern by which superintendents are chosen. Rather, one should determine the approximate size of community he would like to be serving by a certain date. Considerable flexibility should be allowed for in the type of school system, salary range desired, and dates of arriving there. As an opportunity for a new job appears, however, he should measure it against his timetable. If it doesn't fit the over-all pattern, it might be better to decline the opportunity even if it means more money initially. As indicated earlier, one can move too rapidly for the good of his own future. Perhaps the primary criterion by which one should test a move is "Where might this job lead?"

Alternate routes to the eventual goal should be provided. Also, one should not rule out alternate final goals. A man might be shooting for the superintendency of San Francisco as the ultimate objective, but he may discover by the age of forty that he would rather spend the remainder of his life in university teaching, or research, or as a specialized administrator in a sizable school system.

His timetable should provide for various other objectives along the way that will contribute to the final goal as well as to the general satisfactions from life which one has a right to expect. Such objectives would include the arrival of his children, buying a home, insurance plan, and other financial investments, trips, writing articles or a book.

Such an organized way of planning one's life may strike the individual as being cold. It is cold. The romanticist might prefer to glide with the winds and gamble on fate's turning the trick. That, too, is all right. Every person has the right to plan his life as he chooses. The advice here is predicated upon the belief that superintendents want to advance in the profession. A time schedule is merely a device to better the odds for his dreams to materialize.

chapter twelve

Go!

If one were to sound public opinion as to the most powerful influence on American life he would undoubtedly obtain such responses as our legislators, the Supreme Court, the National Association of Manufacturers, organized labor, the church, the farm bloc, the missile builders, or perhaps the devil. Each responder could rally a legion of illustrations in support of his contention. It is unlikely that anyone would mention the superintendents of schools, possibly because it is so obvious, but probably because few persons understand his power.

Scarcely a board member or teacher appreciates fully the impact of the superintendency. If these groups are unaware of the post's importance, it is understandable why laymen would not rate it highly. Most citizens have less understanding about the scope and details of the superintendent's jurisdiction than they do about the fellow who cleans out their clogged sewers. One conscientious and scared superintendent was heard to observe, "If people really knew the extent of authority with which they've entrusted us they'd accompany their kids to school every day."

The logic in the claim for the superintendency's preeminence of influence will resist counterclaims from whatever point the issue is attacked. If one were to assert that war and peace are the two most important forces for a nation's happiness and progress, then we must take our cue from the constitution of UNESCO, "Since wars begin in the minds of men, it is in the minds of men that the defences of peace must be constructed.[1] Following this line of reasoning to its conclusion, we have already seen that the superintendent stands precisely in the strategic position of being able to control concepts which pupils acquire. Since boards of education generally accept the superintendent's recommendations on all school matters to include curriculum content, teaching methods, instructional materials, and selection of teachers, he is in the position to determinine what and how America's future leaders and followers will think.

If one were to argue that the strength lies with citizens of a community who choose members of a board of education, who in turn have legislative authority over the executive, he would be correct insofar as source of power is concerned. However, he would have to admit that the source is alive only with extreme rarity. Few citizens are sufficiently excited about education to exercise their power, and still fewer are willing to accept the legislative responsibility. In reality, therefore, citizens have abrogated their power in favor of the superintendent.

One might cite an earlier observation herein to the effect that authority over public education is vested in the state. While this is legally true, it must be recalled that for the most part, states have delegated their authority to local communities. Thus far, at least, citizens have been much less interested in speaking up about educational matters through their legislators than through their local board members.

Another person might assert that morality, more than reason, governs man's actions. This may be true, though proof will probably never rise above the level of the seminar. Now society has many forces at work to shape one's code of morals: family, church, communication media, organizations, and companions, to name a few. But if one were required to isolate the most singularly important force that influences morality in America, he would have to reduce his choices to

[1] Constitution of the United Nations Educational, Scientific, and Cultural Organization, 1946.

the one agency of society that touches all young people—education, public or private.

All of the other groups and individuals who exert influence on national life, good or evil, wealthy or numerous, must assume a secondary role in view of their dependence upon rational or irrational thinking. Any direction one seeks to trace causal relationships, he finds himself back at control over the mind—exactly where the superintendent operates.

Perhaps society never intended that his role should become one of such sovereignty. If not, citizens cannot abdicate their blame. Superintendents themselves have had little to do with elevating their stature except through becoming professionally trained to handle a technical function. Population growth, too, has enhanced the importance of the position. But the primary reason for this situation is simply that society has abandoned its reponsibility for education at the doorstep marked "Superintendent."

If this assignment of power is misplaced, let us consider the alternatives. Since citizens could shift or reduce the superintendent's power best by changing the local control over public schools, they must start with his immediate superiors, the board of education. The only possible arrangements might be to:

1. Return legislative control over public education to a state level, or perhaps regional or federal.

2. Discontinue boards of education and have the superintendent directly responsible to the entire community. A compromise might be to enlarge the board to fifty or five hundred members in order to assure more direct liaison between superintendent and citizenry.

3. Provide for full-time, technically trained, and paid board members, a sort of board of superintendents rather than just one.

4. Persuade more qualified citizens to become board members.

5. Scrap the public-supported educational system *in toto,* and rebuild a plan of various private schools.

Each of these choices is so fraught with dangers, weaknesses, or implausibilities that a thinking person would give no more than a fleeting consideration to its adoption. Until someone can devise a better workable plan for managing the gigantic enterprise of public education, the strength of America is lodged in the hands of a small division of 14,000 men.

If the present system of control over America's education is the most practical that can be contrived, there can be but one conclusion—the selection and preparation of school superintendents must become a task of the highest priority on the list of society's responsibilities. This is the challenge to the public, to the institutions that prepare school administrators, and to superintendents themselves.

The Challenge to Society

One of the oddest paradoxes in American attitudes is the devoted faith in the ideal of universal education for all children as opposed to the enthusiasm for supporting it. The public desire for educational opportunities is unquestioned; it has almost reached the status of a fanaticism. Every crossroads in the land has made some provision for educating children. In fact, the requirement that United States citizens must educate their children is the one directive they cannot avoid. Men have found ways to avoid all of their obligations which are commonly thought inescapable: obeying the laws of the land, worshiping God, working, voting, owning a home, or paying taxes. But every person, if he remains in this country, must make some provision for educating his children, the only exception being made for a child with a severe handicap which precludes his profiting from an education. And the standard by which the separate provisions are measured if a parent elects not to educate his child in a publicly supported school is that which is offered by the public school.

Notwithstanding the zeal citizens demonstrate for having education, the buildings they have bought for housing pupils, the isolated instances of expressing concern about the educational program, and the cyclical mass apprehension over the quality of training programs, laymen have not manifested interest in, or financial support of, education in any proportion to their desire for having it. For those who begrudge another mill for support of public education and who proclaim the extravagance of educators, they need only be reminded of the mandated importance which citizens have attached to education in relation to the choices they make in the allocation of their income. One needs only to revive the comparative statistics of how people spend for education, the one requirement of all people, and how they spend for homes, clothing, entertainment, automobiles, vacations, highways, armies, funerals, and toothpaste. No intimation is being intended about the rightness and wrongness of this allocation of income. That remains a personal choice. The point being made is the obvious one, that if people hold so dearly the education of children as to decree that goal to the Number One position in their priority of wants, they should back it up with appropriate personal and financial participation. The only recourse is to relieve their chosen representatives, and their employed professional personnel, from the responsibility for achieving the impossible.

This is the challenge before American citizens regarding their educational programs—to decide whether they actually mean that they want mandated universal education. If not, a completely new approach to educating youth may be launched. If, on the other hand, the idea is to be perpetuated, the desire must be expressed in a vastly more tangible way than witnessed thus far. The numerous debates that rage periodically about portions of the educational program, about teaching techniques, or philosophy, are of no more consequence than selecting the kind of nails for building a house. The nature of the house must be decided upon first.

If society chooses to preserve its ideal of universal education that is peculiar to this nation, and decides further that it is worth its cost, and if it can find no better structure for conducting the enterprise, then it has some sub-challenges on hand. It has the challenge of seeking out its most able representatives to place in the one spot where the structure permits vigorous influence on education—the superintendency. This means the further challenge of giving serious thought to the selection of well-qualified members for the board of education. It also means answering the challenge of *how* to persuade able representatives to consider school administration as a career. This answer requires no great imagination in a society that holds material gain on such a high plane.

There is the additional challenge before citizens of devoting whatever time and effort is needed to understand better the operations of public education, specifically the *modus operandi* of their superintendent, his authority, and function. If there be a flickering doubt about the general lack of concern for the superintendent's work, it can be confirmed by a quick perusal of the popular periodicals, those organs which are supposed to reflect public reader interest. One can find articles in the "slicks" on nearly every other phase of society's business, sordid or solid. One can even read about many educational activities: the football team, the teacher shortage, the difficulty of getting into college, the band, educational shortcomings, the handicapped child, crowded schools, or youthful misdeeds. But one is asked to recall when he last saw an article in a popular magazine about the fellow who is responsible for it all—the superintendent.

When citizens understand this office, they can quickly rectify the conditions which throttle the superintendents' attempts to provide good educational programs for their children. Undoubtedly their first act will be to assure that their school system obtains the caliber of man needed for the job. Secondly,

they will provide enough assistants to relieve him from the
housekeeping chores so that he may be freed to perform the
leadership role they have a right to expect. They are entitled
to demand top performance and production from this officer,
but not without the tools and assistance needed by any executive. Other needed changes will then fall into line, hastily and
in an orderly way.

The Challenge to Administrator-Training Institutions

If the public should ever accept the challenge outlined in
the previous lines, as they certainly must soon, universities that
undertake to prepare administrators have thrust upon them
immediately a challenge of almost equal importance, though
easier of attainment. Their challenge involves program, facilities, and staff. If society manages to steer its ablest men into
the school administrative profession, universities must be
ready to provide its finest preparation, qualitatively and quanti-
tatively.

Even without the degree of public support of education
as required by public expectations, the need for quality leadership of schools in the remainder of this century is greater than
heretofore experienced. Assuming no change in public attitude
toward education, there will be more children to educate at
all levels than have yet rapped on school doors. There will
unquestionably be some additional or different demands made
upon schools as a result of the current national concern. Regardless of how the wind of public reaction blows, superintendents will be called upon to be better financial managers,
more efficient organizers, sharper salesmen, more adroit
speakers, keener students of human motivation and of community interaction, better curriculum leaders, and more stoic
stoics. This is the challenge of the universities.

There is little wrong with the administrative-training programs that a realistic appraisal of the superintendent's job

wouldn't cure. One possible program has already been outlined in Chapter 11 and will not be enlarged upon here. Undoubtedly, further refinements could be developed with united
effort of administration professors and as changing conditions
warrant. Perhaps the greatest obstacles to overcome are oppositional philosophies, the tenacious grip of university hierarchy and liberal arts devotees upon the meaning of a Doctor's
degree, and attracting adequate and qualified instructors.

The past decade has witnessed some unprecedented efforts
on the part of professors of educational administration in
pooling talents to improve the training program. For the first
time in history, a rather sizable quantity of money has been
made available specifically to inquire into the nature of school
administration in order to develop a conformable preparatory
program. The efforts of the University Council of Educational Administration and the National Conference of Professors of Education Administration are praiseworthy in their
spirit of research and in their tabulation of findings to date.
Whether or not the current search for an illusive administrative theory—a sort of promising formula with which administrators in training can be inoculated—will be productive can
only be determined with more time and study. It is hoped that
the search does not end in research for the sake of research,
in scholarly exercises to establish personal, departmental, or
institutional status, or in a packet of principles irrelevant to
the real function of administrative practitioners.

University departments of educational administration have
a further challenge of stepping up their technical service to
administrators "in the field." Already great strides have been
made in this direction by individual efforts and through the
various service bureaus sponsored by many universities. Their
facilities for research, surveys, and professional counsel, though
shackled by a dearth of financial resources and by overbur-
dened personnel, have provided considerable technical aid to
school districts in need of help. However, a reorientation of
purpose may be called for toward a stronger recognition that

a university which proposes to serve the nation's schools has a continuing responsibility beyond the initial training of teachers and administrators. One rich field where the first furrow has yet to be turned is in the challenge to devise a system for bringing the most talented forces to bear in helping school administrators to put out the various fires that start in school districts.

The Challenge to Superintendents

The challenge presented practicing and future superintendents is the most thrilling of all. It is simply the dare to fulfill society's expectations.

The winning of this challenge entails three important accomplishments. The first is to become completely and professionally trained to do the job. Nothing less than the acquisition of all the know-how about the job will suffice. The time is not far away when eligibility for obtaining a superintendency post will be established by the completion of a doctoral degree. The first courageous step has already been taken by practicing administrators themselves when, at their 1959 Atlantic City convention of the American Association of School Administrators, they voted more than two to one to require the attainment of two years of graduate professional training in order to qualify for future membership in that organization.

The initial preparation is not the end of the line. In order to live up to the expectations, and in order to qualify as the new modern brand of superintendent, they must keep abreast of developments, research, and techniques. This is an endless task. And when society lives up to its end of the bargain, administrators will have time for further study.

A second accomplishment needed to discharge their expectations is to shore up their weaknesses in those areas suggested herein. They must reappraise their effectiveness with staff, board members, and citizens to see if they can adapt the techniques employed by successful superintendents. Because of the nature of their work that involves three-fourths human relations, and because this is the skill that tests most of their success, it is in this area that superintendents must exert the greatest improvement.

Superintendents have a further challenge, shared also by universities, in aiding society to recognize and meet its challenge to education. Most citizens are not aware of the major decision with which they are confronted; others who recognize it would prefer to evade the decision. People generally would rather postpone the trip to the dentist as long as the tooth doesn't hurt too much. It has been argued at times that the same attitude might be applied to corrective measures for education. If one waits long enough the tooth may rot, and if citizens delay long enough their schools might deteriorate. "Let them close," some have said, "and then the public will face up to its charge." This point of view would be defensible if no more than a toothache were at stake. But as the financial support behind each child becomes increasingly less, the lives of thousands of young men and women constitute the pawn. The sacrifice of this talent and manpower is too great a price to pay for lethargy.

Since the majority of citizens will not face the issue voluntarily, educators and board members must focus public attention on the inevitable decision—persistently, tactfully, and surely.

Never before in the history of educational endeavor has the future held forth such an onerous but rewarding challenge as that awaiting the superintendents of America. Never has there been a greater need for hardy men. A powerful force with a vital mission awaits capable reinforcements.